# HOW TO BE A
# DOMESTIC
# GODDESS

# HOW TO BE A
# DOMESTIC
# GODDESS

**MAEVE BRADBURY AND
JENNIFER WORICK**

APPLE

First published in the UK in 2008 by
Apple Press
7 Greenland Street
London
NW1 0ND
www.apple-press.com

Copyright © Elwin Street Limited 2008

Conceived and produced by
Elwin Street Limited
144 Liverpool Road
London N1 1LA
www.elwinstreet.com

ISBN 978-1-84543-247-8

Designed by Sharanjit Dhol
Illustrations by David Eaton
Picture credits: all from Getty Images

10 9 8 7 6 5 4 3 2 1

Printed in Singapore

# CONTENTS

# INTRODUCTION

My mother is one of the few people I know who actually uses fish knives and forks and jam spoons, who can sense dust in unseen places and cares, who vacuums under her bed and who knows how to get bicycle grease out of silk lampshades . . . She is the Ultimate Domestic Goddess. And she manages to make it look both elegant and easy at the same time.

For a long time I resisted my mother's influence, deliberately doing totally uncivilised things like putting the milk bottle directly onto the table rather than decanting into a jug. It all seemed too much like hard work and rather old-fashioned in this post-feminist era.

So as a young woman, my home was chaotic and disorganised, and dare I say it, perhaps a little on the grubby side. Mountains of dirty laundry threatened to overwhelm the house, the fridge was empty and the vacuum cleaner broken. I was late for everything because I always had to hunt for a missing shoe or important paperwork. Slowly but surely, it dawned on me – there had to be a better way.

There is. Becoming a Domestic Goddess means taking control of your life. The undisputed mistress of the house, an accomplished cook and a perfect hostess, the Domestic Goddess can handle anything and knows it. Her confidence is absolute, her accomplishments legendary . . . or so it seems. It's all about making it look effortless – it's really just a frame of mind, involving 10 per cent perspiration and 90 per cent attitude. You need to know how to avoid letting the housework take over your life, leaving you with plenty of time to get your hair done, redecorate the spare room or take a night-class in astrophysics.

This book will show you how to become a celebrated hostess, cook like a top-class chef, keep your house welcoming and live in domestic bliss. Not only does a Domestic Goddess know exactly how to dress and behave whatever the occasion, she appears to sail through life with an air of collected calm. No social event can knock her off her guard and no domestic catastrophe can make her lose her cool. She is prepared for every eventuality – from an interfering mother-in-law to the arrival of unexpected guests, a missing button or a fallen hem, an empty store cupboard or a stain on the carpet – she takes it all in her high-heeled stride.

If you thought like I did that taking pride in your home was a rather outdated pre-occupation, think again – I am not advocating a return to the days when our mothers were shackled to the kitchen sink and a woman's place was firmly in the home. This is modern domesticity for the twenty-first century woman, who still wants to be able to return to a habitable home in the evenings. The information in this book will help you to take control of your home, your life, your family and yourself. Packed with advice, helpful checklists and charts, multi-tasking and time-saving tips and shortcuts, this is the handbook for every aspiring superwoman. So if you feel that your housekeeping skills leave a little to be desired, your domestic accomplishments need some fine tuning and your presentation requires a little polish, read on.

# LOOKING
# AND
# ACTING
# THE
# PART

A Domestic Goddess knows how to maintain a calm and efficient home and at the same time remain unflustered, polite and, most importantly, ravishingly glamorous no matter what the day throws at her.

# LOOKING THE PART

As a Domestic Goddess you know that looking the part is an essential part of your goddess status, that must be maintained at all times. Just because you may have to get your hands a little dirty around the house, doesn't mean you should ever conjure up such ghastly images as nylon housecoats, rubber gloves and hairnets, or down-at-heel slippers and bleach-stained tracksuit bottoms. That said, even the most glamorous woman knows she has to put in some work to maintain that goddess-like appearance. A wash-and-go haircut and a streamlined morning routine will make your life a lot easier, but everyday maintenance is essential to maintain your allure. Unfortunately, you are not a fine wine – you won't improve with age or neglect.

## WAR PAINT

Putting on your make-up and doing your hair should be part of your morning ritual. You don't need full war-paint and a shampoo-and-set every day, but a good brushing, some light moisturising foundation, a lick of mascara and lip gloss, will have you feeling presentable. It is also much nicer for everyone who has to look at you. Keep your nails short and use a pale or clear varnish, so chips will not be noticeable. It's a good idea to keep a comb, lip gloss and loose powder by the hall mirror, for emergency touch-ups in case you have to answer the door.

## KEEPING UP APPEARANCES

Make time in your busy schedule for trips to the hairdresser and beauty salon. Falling into a rut will cause you to become complacent with your grooming and perhaps even your romantic life. Even the simplest act of buying a lipstick in a new colour can feel like a little indulgence for yourself.

## MAKEOVER MAGIC

Get regular makeovers at your favourite department store. Keep up on the latest looks, don't be afraid to try new ones, and treat yourself by adding a new eye-shadow or cream blush to your collection occasionally. Remember, make-up products don't last forever, so you'll probably end up replacing certain items like mascara even if the tube isn't completely finished.

Do not submit to a whole new trend when revamping your look. Just incorporate one fresh element to keep up-to-date. Make-up should always bring out your natural beauty and enhance it, not act as a mask. A simple rule is to just emphasise one feature. If you concentrate on your eyes for instance, keep your lipstick light. If you opt for a strong colour on your mouth, your eye make-up should be more subtle.

## LUSCIOUS LIPS

Keep a lipstick in each of your handbags, in the glove compartment of your car, and in the bathroom and you will never again be caught off-guard. A colourful lipstick will give you a polished look, no matter how bare the rest of your face is. It is a good idea also to keep a small mirror and make-up kit in your kitchen. If you are hosting a dinner party, or watching the big game on TV with The Husband's chums, freshen up by the refrigerator between courses or while fetching more beer.

## BATTLE DRESS

It makes sense to wear comfortable and practical clothing – save the frills and flounces for going out – but that doesn't mean letting yourself go. A good rule of thumb is to imagine that your ex-lover might ring the doorbell at any given moment. If you can confidently open the door and know that he will swoon at the apparition before him, you are ready to face the day – and any unexpected visitors.

It is perfectly permissible to keep a set of 'working' clothes – an old shirt of The Husband's or a cute set of denim overalls worn with attitude can look quite sexy in the right circumstances. Usually this requires a paintbrush or trowel to complete your outfit. However, don't be tempted to nip out to the shops. The ex-lover will have chosen that exact moment to pick up some groceries and the effect will be lost. To be on the safe side, if you can get someone in to do the decorating and to mow your lawn, this problem will never occur.

## KIT AND CABOODLE

There are certain rather unglamorous accessories that will be needed to get the job done. You may think you can shun such items as an apron, but it is an essential piece of kit that will save you from having to change outfits every time you splash a sauce down your top – not a good look for a Goddess. Needless to say, you should never leave the house in your apron.

Rubber gloves are particularly unattractive, but they are, unfortunately, incredibly useful. Unpleasant tasks, if you must do them – such as cleaning the bathroom and unblocking drains – are not comfortably done without them. It might be best to make sure the house is empty when you wear them and you're not expecting any callers. Be quick, get the job done and take them off as soon as possible. Keep some hand-cream next to the sink to slather on as soon as you have finished to make you feel better.

## *A Domestic Goddess Would Never . . .*

[X]  Emphasise both lips and eyes. Choose your most alluring features and delicately enhance them.

[X]  Heavily powder her face. Looking like a snowman will not do; a little spot of powder on a shiny nose will suffice.

[X]  Reapply her make-up in a public area. Ever.

[X]  Neglect her nails. Make sure you treat yourself to regular manicures, keep your nails neat and always remove all traces of nail varnish once it has started to chip.

[X]  Allow a tangerine tinge to colour her face. There is seldom anything more ridiculous than a woman who looks like she has been dunked in orange paint. If in doubt, seek the advice of instore experts to help you choose the shade that suits you.

[X]  Be a slave to trends. Seek out cosmetics and styles that enhance your unique beauty.

[X]  Forget to remove her make-up before retiring to bed. No matter how tired you may feel, smeared mascara on your face and pillow is never attractive.

[X]  Allow any form of facial hair to remain visible. Moustaches, stray whiskers and nose hair must be removed at once. Never ever mention their existence.

# EVERYDAY ELEGANCE

Looking the part isn't just important for your Goddess image – looking and feeling your best helps to make light work of housework. If you feel fabulous, you'll attack those household chores with a spring in your step. Think of taking care of yourself, and a little pampering every now and again, as an essential part of your household duties. Maintaining your everyday elegance does require some careful forethought and planning. No matter how much time you may spend getting ready in the mornings, it is difficult to retain a look of poised perfection throughout the day when you are hot and bothered. So keep the windows open when doing onerous tasks, wear loose comfortable clothing, drink plenty of water and sit down frequently. Better still, delegate all strenuous jobs!

## PREPARATION AND PLANNING

Don't forget to keep your wardrobe maintained. Don't put anything away in your closet unless it is clean, ironed and ready to put on. Sew buttons on the moment they fall off; mend rips and tears, uneven hems and fraying seams when you notice them – though you may not choose to spend your own time on such tasks, so always keep the number of a good seamstress to hand. If you keep on top of these simple things, you will always be able to get ready at a moment's notice, confident you look your well-dressed best.

It is always useful to have some tried-and-tested outfits in mind, in case The Husband calls and wants to take you out for dinner when he gets home, or you are invited to a function at short notice. This prevents hours spent standing before the mirror, in the vain hope of finding something to wear that miraculously makes both your bottom and waist look smaller, your breasts larger, and your legs longer.

## ADD ACCESSORIES

Clever use of accessories can lift your outfit and make you look groomed and glamorous, even if you are just wearing your jeans. Invest in a smart, leather handbag and team with a pair of boots when you go out. The rule with jewellery is to not overdo it. Choose a few reliable items for your everyday signature, such as discreet earrings, so that you always look polished and perfectly accessorised. Large hooped earrings will make you look like a fortune teller, as will too much jewellery in general – particularly gold. Keep it simple and save your baubles for going out.

## GETTING IT RIGHT

There is a very thin line between appearing vulgar and making a witty statement with your clothes. If you are not sure where the line is, it is probably better to avoid certain, potentially disastrous, fashion items. There is really nothing worse than thinking you are at the cutting-edge of sartorial trend, when actually you look like a fashion-victim. The old saying that a girl's clothes should be 'tight enough to know she's a woman, but loose enough to know she's a lady' is a useful guide.

Remember that natural fabrics work best. Synthetic material, particularly nylon and acrylic, can have the most alarming habit of attracting static and preventing your skin from breathing properly, not to mention collecting an impressive quantity of fluff and giving little electric shocks to anyone who brushes past.

Above all, you should never be a slave to fashion. You need to be able to keep you look up-to-date, without falling victim to every trend that sashays down the catwalk. The trick is to carry off a look that simultaneously suggests that you care about your appearance, but that there was no effort involved in the process at all. Honestly.

## LESS IS MORE!

Elegance is all about stylish understatement. It is also about knowing how to dress appropriately for the occasion. Wearing an eye-popping killer dress is not going to endear yourself to the in-laws when you are invited for tea. A helpful rule is to emphasise only one of your physical assets at a time. If you have great legs, wear a pretty short skirt – an inch or so above the knee is quite short enough, thank you – but don't match it with a low-cut top. If you have a marvellous decolletage, unbutton your blouse slightly, but team it with a modest pair of tailored trousers. Remember – less is more!

| If you like your | Wear |
| --- | --- |
| Ample bosom | V-neck blouses |
| Small bosom | A defined bodice, such as a delicate empire-line top |
| Toned arms | 3/4-length sleeves, halter tops |
| Flat stomach | Low-rise waistbands, snug knit tops |
| Boyish hips | A-line skirts |
| Tiny bottom | Form-fitting trousers or jeans |
| Hourglass figure | Pencil-line skirts, fitted sheath dresses |
| Petite frame | Skirts and dresses that hit above the knee |
| Slim legs | Short but not-too-short skirt |
| Slim waist | Fitted dresses and coats with belts |

| If you don't care for your | Wear |
| --- | --- |
| Thick arms | Long sleeves |
| Belly | High-waisted dresses or tunic tops |
| Big bottom | Long-flowing skirts |
| Child-bearing hips | Flat-front trousers with no pockets |
| Thick thighs | Generous cut trousers |
| Ample bosom | Round-necked tops in dark colours |
| Small bosom | Bosom-enhancing bras and tops |

# ACTING THE PART

Being a Domestic Goddess is all about attitude. This is particularly true when it comes to acting the part. The Husband doesn't always appreciate just how hard you work on his behalf, but there are ways to keep your chin up and your smile fixed at all times.

## RESPECT YOURSELF

Whether you have to do the cleaning and washing yourself, or you have someone to do it for you, it is normally the woman of the house who organises its running. This is your domain and you are in charge. Insist that you are given the respect you deserve. Without you there would be chaos, and world leaders would be turning up to international summits wearing odd socks and dirty underpants, having breakfasted on left-over cold pizza.

## SMILE AND FAKE IT

If you're finding it difficult to keep on top of things, the best thing to do is pretend you're in control. If you appear cool and confident, organised and super-efficient, other people will believe that you actually are (including The Husband). Never flap and never panic. Practise looking calm and serene. Your biggest weapon is a smile. When faced with a difficult situation (a rude, ill-mannered person, a bill you cannot pay, an appointment you have missed, or a dinner that has burnt, to name just a few trials a you may be forced to face in her day), play for time and smile sweetly. It creates a sense that none of life's little crises can burst your bubble of good-humoured efficiency. You may be dying of embarrassment inside and wishing the ground would swallow you up, but no-one will know. Act as if you are completely in control, even when you don't feel it, and sooner or later you will have convinced everyone how capable you are. More importantly, you will start to believe it yourself.

# PERFECT GUEST

Being a perfect guest is essential so that you are always inundated with invitations to keep your social calendar full. You need to know just how to behave at any social function, event or party.

## A Perfect Guest Knows...

- ✓ It's polite to bring a bottle of wine for your hostess, or some small gesture of appreciation, such as flowers.

- ✗ Don't monopolise your host or hostess, as they must circulate and talk to all their guests.

- ✓ Have the confidence to approach strangers and introduce yourself, initiate conversations with people you don't know and help to get the party off to a jolly start.

- ✗ It is very rude to gaze over someone's shoulder when they are talking, as if you were scanning the room for someone far more interesting – even if you have got stuck with a crashing old bore!

- ✗ Never bring a friend to a party without having asked the hostess first. Even if you are certain that she won't object, make sure you call her first to check, and don't press the point if she demurs.

- ✗ Don't overstay your welcome! Take your cue from the other guests and when people start to drift away, it is time to leave too.

- ✓ Seek out your host and hostess before you go and remember to thank them very much for an enjoyable evening.

- ✓ It is a nice touch to send a thank you note the following day, unless it was an informal party, in which case a quick telephone call will suffice.

# GETTING ORGANISED

Writing lists is one of the best ways to keep track of what's happening in your immensely busy life. If you get into the habit of keeping a To Do list, divided into immediate tasks and long-term projects, you'll be able to keep on top of your responsibilities. Tackle your job like a military campaign. If you approach it with an attitude of importance, other people will respond in the same way.

## ORGANISING THE HUSBAND

Unfortunately nature has seen fit to endow only women with the life-skill of multi-tasking. This means that your beloved does not have room in his head for more than one thing at a time. He will forget the simplest of requests, the easiest of chores so that if you ask him to buy some milk from the shop after he has picked up the kids from school and dropped off your dry-cleaning, the chances are he will arrive back at home with either your children or the milk, and possibly your dirty laundry too.

### *Taking Control of The Husband*

☑ If you're sending him out to run errands, write down the list of things he supposed to be doing or getting. He may well lose it the moment he steps out of the door, but at least you will have done all you can.

☑ A family calendar is one of the most useful tools you can have when getting The Husband organised. Pin the largest one you can find up in the kitchen where he can clearly see it.

☑ Write absolutely everything on it – from birthdays to dental appointments, from school outings to business meetings. If the plumber is due to fix the leaky tap, write it down. If his mother telephoned, write it down. If the car needs servicing, write it down.

☑ It may help to colour code the entries; one for his reminders, one for yours, and one for the extremely urgent you-absolutely-must-not-forget-about-this reminders, so he can clearly see what he is supposed to be doing.

☑ Get him into the habit of recording on the calendar all of his important dates and appointments as well so you don't have to monitor his diary quite so carefully for him.

☑ You will probably still have to regularly remind him to check the calendar, but this should start to jog his memory. It will also remind him of how much you do to keep his life running smoothly.

# EVERYDAY MANNERS

It goes without saying that a Domestic Goddess has beautiful manners. Not only do you know how to dress appropriately for any occasion, you also know exactly how to behave, and can always be thoughtful, courteous and polite, whatever the situation.

Good manners really means showing due consideration to others. While social codes of conduct may be less rigorous now, customs less complicated and more flexible, it doesn't mean that you can spit with impunity. Good manners help to oil the cogs of civilised interaction. If this doesn't come naturally to you, it helps to follow a few basic principles.

## BASIC MANNERS

An awful lot can be achieved just by remembering to say 'Please' and 'Thank you' at the appropriate moments. It works even better, as most things do, if accompanied by a smile. Hold the door open for everyone, male or female. On buses and trains, offer your seat to older people. Be kind to children and animals.

## CONVERSATION

Avoid topics of conversation that may cause offence or embarrassment. This includes discussing intimate details about most things – illnesses you may suffer from and sexual practices you may indulge in, for example. It is probably best not to ask anyone their age, unless you are fairly sure they are pre-adolescent. Never enquire how much someone earns – this is the height of rudeness. In fact, it is safer to avoid discussing the subject of money with anyone. Sex is a topic best kept to your own bedroom, and Religion and Politics are equally off-limits. The idea is to talk only about things which are inoffensive and which everyone can participate in. This really only leaves the weather.

## FLIRTING

As a Domestic Goddess, you know you come into your own on the subject of flirting! In fact, there is little you can do better – except, perhaps, pipe sugar icing into miniature roses or remove mildew from frosted glass shower screens. A well-timed glance over your shoulder, or a bashful flutter of your eyelashes, ensures the greengrocer supplies you with the freshest vegetables. It speeds up many of the tedious processes that accompany daily life, helping to smooth over dealings with tradesmen and shopkeepers, bank managers and bus conductors, and results in a first-class service.

It doesn't do to be too obvious; there should be just enough to intrigue the majority of men whose egos are located in their trousers. Cultivate an air of vulnerability, and practise lowering your head and looking up through your eyelashes. Don't be tempted to unbutton your blouse to the waist or shorten your skirts. That signals an availability which might confuse your audience, especially if you only wish to jump the queue at the supermarket.

## USING THE TELEPHONE

It is extremely inconsiderate to call anyone before 9 o'clock in the morning or after 9 o'clock at night, unless it is someone with whom you are familiar enough to know their daily routine. Even then, it might be wiser not to call anyone outside these hours, except for close girlfriends or your mother.

If you wish to terminate a telephone conversation early, there are tactful ways of bringing it to a close. 'Well, it was lovely to talk to you, but I mustn't keep you' or 'I could go on chatting with you forever, but I have a doctor's appointment in half an hour'. If these approaches fail, tell them that you must go as someone is at the door. As a last resort, make crackling noises into the telephone, or turn the coffee-maker on and hold the receiver next to it. Shout 'The line is breaking up!' and put the phone down.

# 2

# MAINTAINING THE HUSBAND

Maintaining the Husband is as much part of a Domestic Goddess's role as maintaining the home. He needs the same care and attention as your house, if not more. A happy husband makes for a happy wife, so it is in your interests to approach your relationship with the due diligence that you show to your domestic duties. Be his companion, his rock, his best friend, his lover; you will maintain a happy husband and he will reciprocate.

# MAKE HIM FEEL LIKE A MAN

A wife who understands that her husband's identity is bound up in his masculinity will strive to keep him feeling like a man. Let him at least think that he wears the proverbial trousers in your twosome. Cede manly tasks, like repairing the roof or fixing a leaky tap, to him. Why, he'll puff up like a blowfish if you ask him to do a simple task like check the air pressure on your tyres! You know you could do these tasks yourself if you really wanted to, but why break a sweat or a nail when you have a perfectly good man in need of a little ego-stroking? When he heads to the garage with a tyre gauge, you can spend that time doing something much more interesting.

## KING OF THE CASTLE

Give him a chance to feel as if he is master of his domain. Carve out an area, be it the garage or the study, where he is king. Let him organise and decorate it the way he wants. Let him rule in certain areas about which you don't care and ones at which he'll excel. These may be traditional male bastions like mechanics or landscaping, or he might shine in historically female arenas, such as sewing, gardening or cooking. Hold your tongue if he does anything you dislike (within reason of course). Just turn your attention to the other areas of your home.

## GIRLY GLAMOUR

When it comes to dressing, why not dress to accentuate his best features from time to time? Wear flats to accentuate his height. Slip into dresses and skirts to complement his inherent manliness. Spritz on a floral perfume and slick on a shimmery lip gloss. A Domestic Goddess never forgets her femininity and he will admire your female form!

## GET WHAT YOU DESERVE

Understanding your needs should be high on The Husband's list of priorities. Be sure to let him know what you expect, not by force or nagging, but with subtle hints and perhaps by offering your own rewards in return. Not feeling the love and appreciation you deserve can only lead to resentment, unhappiness and disaster!

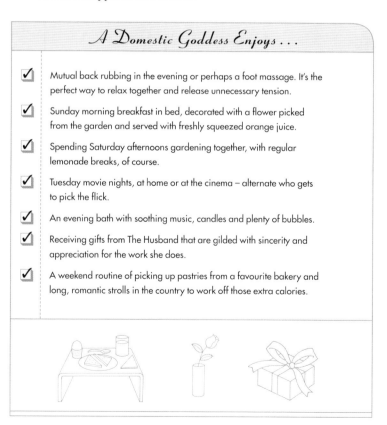

### A Domestic Goddess Enjoys . . .

- ✓ Mutual back rubbing in the evening or perhaps a foot massage. It's the perfect way to relax together and release unnecessary tension.

- ✓ Sunday morning breakfast in bed, decorated with a flower picked from the garden and served with freshly squeezed orange juice.

- ✓ Spending Saturday afternoons gardening together, with regular lemonade breaks, of course.

- ✓ Tuesday movie nights, at home or at the cinema – alternate who gets to pick the flick.

- ✓ An evening bath with soothing music, candles and plenty of bubbles.

- ✓ Receiving gifts from The Husband that are gilded with sincerity and appreciation for the work she does.

- ✓ A weekend routine of picking up pastries from a favourite bakery and long, romantic strolls in the country to work off those extra calories.

# KEEP HIM ON HIS TOES . . .

A subtle way to guarantee that he never takes you for granted is to cultivate an air of mystery. Don't apprise him of your schedule unless he asks and then only keep to the specific query at hand. Be a little vague – certainly don't bore him with a list of all the household chores you'll be doing that day.

## CLOSE THE DOOR

You may share a bathroom, but there is no need for him to be familiar with the more unglamorous aspects of your beauty regime. Close the door when using the lavatory, bleaching your upper lip or shaving your legs. You want to make everything seem effortless – including looking like a goddess every day. He doesn't need to know the lengths to which us girls have to go, to remain smooth, polished and fragrant.

## SURPRISE HIM!

Occasionally, pay him unexpected visits during the day to deliver his lunch or drop off a note. Each visit should have a purpose – don't just drop by his office to say hello or he may feel like you are checking up on him rather than running a thoughtful errand or delivering a loving message.

## BECOME HIS 'WORK-MATE'

Take a real interest in his work. It's surprising how many people don't have a clear idea of what their partner does all day. Read up on his field through the Internet, books or professional journals he leaves lying about. Ask him questions. Ask him about his specialist areas of law, finance, construction – whatever – and get to know the names of his key co-workers. Most probably, he will love sharing this important area of his life with you. If you get into the habit of discussing his day, he won't feel the slightest need to turn to someone else who 'understands' what he goes through from nine to five.

# ... BUT DON'T SMOTHER HIM

Your husband is with you because he wants to be. After all, you are a Domestic Goddess! Trust that. Asking for reassurance, calling him frequently at work, wanting to spend every waking moment with him are casebook techniques almost guaranteed to drive him away, perhaps into the arms of another woman.

Give him a bit of space so he thinks he has a modicum of free will. Saccharine as it may seem, there is some truth to the adage that if you love someone, set him free. If he comes back to you, he's yours. If he doesn't, he never belonged to you.

## *Give Him Space*

- ✓ Encourage him to get together with his friends for poker nights or outings to the local pub.

- ✓ Read a book in bed or take a bath while he watches television in the living room.

- ✓ Support him if he wants to take a trip with his friends, family, or an organisation or club.

- ✓ Bring him dinner on a tray if he's working on a project in the garage or basement.

- ✓ Allow him to subscribe to whatever magazines he chooses, no matter how prurient.

- ✓ Surprise him by performing one of his allotted tasks or errands and let him have that time to himself.

# TRAINING THE HUSBAND

Every woman has heard it before. The Husband forgot to take out the rubbish . . . again. This is understandably irritating, but on no account should you throw in the towel and accept defeat!

## HOUSE-TRAINING.

Training a man is like training a small child or a puppy, although it should be a lot less messy. The secret is positive reinforcement. When first setting up house, split the chores. Post a list on the refrigerator where he can see it. Offer him special prizes or incentives for jobs well done. Praise him, thank him, show him how grateful you are when he does remember to do his share. He will feel appreciated and will enjoy making you happy and so will learn to do it again!

## GOOD BOY!

Don't let things fester. But don't jump on him if you've been stewing all day because he forgot to take out the rubbish . . . again. Give him a chance to unwind and maybe remember on his own. Don't wait for him to slip up – if he continues to forget, help him to remember by leaving him casual notes.

## PATIENCE IS A VIRTUE.

Sigh . . . so what if you live with a slob? Unfortunately, you may well have to accept his slovenly behaviour – but that doesn't mean you have to live in a pigsty. Make it easy for him to be clean. Place laundry bins around the bedroom and bathroom and lots of rubbish bins around the house. If you resent picking up after The Husband, give him other tasks that even out the workload in your mind. Picking up the children, handling the bills and maintaining the cars can all help lessen the feeling that you are running a one-woman maid service.

## *Positive Reinforcement*

| **H E . . .** | **Y O U . . .** |
|---|---|
| **1** Does the taxes | **1** Do the dishes for a month |
| **2** Fixes a clogged drain | **2** Make breakfast in bed |
| **3** Washes the car | **3** Prepare his favourite dish |
| **4** Cleans the gutters | **4** Pay for a romantic night out |
| **5** Cleans out the garage | **5** Clean out the wardrobes |
| **6** Takes out the rubbish | **6** Caddy for him on 18 holes of golf |
| **7** Washes the dog | **7** Buy him tickets for a sports event |

# AVOID NAGGING

Many women channel their frustration with an errant partner by vigorously throwing themselves into the housework. They give their husband the silent treatment while they scrub the grout in the bath. It's always important to remember at this point that he can't read your mind! If you are peeved that he didn't remember to wash the car or pick up the dry-cleaning, don't expect him to figure out his memory lapse on his own.

Stop. Take a deep breath. Pretend someone is zipping you into a really tight-fitting dress and hold it. Slowly release. Do this as many times as need be until adrenalin stops coursing through your body and your complexion has returned to its normal hue. That's better. Now, there are two courses of action: preventative and counter measures.

## Preventative Measures

☑ Agree which jobs are yours and which are his. If you establish this right from the beginning, he will know what is expected of him.

☑ Give each other space and spend time apart. It isn't good for your relationship or your sanity to spend every waking moment together.

☑ Give plenty of positive reinforcement!

☑ Be patient – reconditioning your husband may take some time, but with you to guide him, he'll get there eventually.

## Counter Measures

☑ Choose your battles wisely. You will lose the impact if you chide him for everything, both large and small.

☑ Don't attack him or go on the offensive. Instead, explain how his behaviour makes you feel.

☑ Don't keep things bottled up. Try having a rational discussion rather than suppressing your emotions. Otherwise you are likely to blow your top!

☑ Be kind. Don't patronise or use sarcasm or he will raise his defensive shield.

☑ Keep it light. You don't want to scare him, so use humour where appropriate to keep it from turning into a drama.

☑ Don't retaliate. He doesn't disappoint you deliberately, in fact he is probably quite bewildered by the need to put the lavatory seat down. Don't be tempted to forgo your own responsibilities to spite him. He probably wouldn't notice anyway.

# KEEPING COOL

It goes without saying that you are a well-bred lady and would never dream of hitting anyone, least of all the love of your life. Of course there are countless times when you may want to. However much he may frustrate and annoy you at times, remember, The Husband does love you. He is simply experiencing an unfortunate lack of judgement. This will pass. It goes without saying that you should not pout or sulk. There isn't much point anyway as, unlike women, men can't seem to equate a dour expression with a bad mood. Take deep breaths and make yourself feel better imagining all those things you would never really do.

## A Domestic Goddess Would Never ...

- ✓ Cut discreet holes in his clothes so that he only realises when it's too late.
- ✓ Make a dish he is allergic to.
- ✓ Keep replacing the batteries in the TV remote with drained ones.
- ✓ Tell his pals about his sexual preferences.
- ✓ Add Tabasco to his coffee and hide fish entrails in his shoes.
- ✓ Replace his shaving cream with whipped cream.
- ✓ Deliberately scratch his car and blame it on youth crime.
- ✓ Set all the clocks an hour fast and watch him panic in the morning.
- ✓ Ritually burn his entire film collection and auction off his first edition books in aid of charity.
- ✓ Replace his work suit with an identical one that is two sizes too small.

# RULE THE BEDROOM

If the only thing you are worried about in the bedroom department is his pile of dirty clothes on the floor and the fact he steals the duvet, that's great. Given time, you can train him to put his laundry in the basket and buy a larger eiderdown. However, your individual sex drives will speed up and slow down at different times. With stress, change, hectic schedules and biorhythms cropping up, it is to be expected that you won't be cruising down the freeway of love without stalling on a pothole or two.

Routine can be a problem. You probably know the benefit of spontaneity and innovation in your sex life, but you may be out of ideas. Do you feel as if the mystery has gone from your relationship every time he walks in on you while you're taking a bath? Perhaps it's time to take steps to ensure that you and The Husband are not in this situation for long.

## TAKE ACTION BEFORE THE SIZZLE FIZZLES

It may feel awkward to outright ask him about his sexual preferences, but this is a good way to spice up your sex life with some new ideas. If you are shy about the direct approach, look for clues, such as groaning and heavy breathing during sex. This indicates a high level of arousal, which in turn indicates that he likes what you are doing. If he holds you in place, continue what you're doing. If he gives you verbal cues or encouragement, stay the course. On the other hand, if he's unresponsive, quiet, and calm, you may want to switch gears. If you are unable to decipher his body language or guttural noises, it's time to gather concrete information directly from the source. There are ways to ask him questions without seeming crude or indelicate. Do not interrogate him in one long session; you may overwhelm him, just focus on one or two questions when he is relaxed or his guard is down.

# KEEP HIM GUESSING

Make an effort to change things every now and again. You don't want him to take you – and your needs – for granted. If there is one position you revere above all others, be careful not to direct him to it every time you have sex. Similarly, don't get stuck in a rut over the time of day you have sex or the frequency in which you engage in the pleasure principle.

If you love foreplay, try skipping it sometime and get straight down to business. If you like morning sex, bring him breakfast in bed instead and spend the evening frolicking between the sheets.

Keep him in a perpetual state of anticipation over your next racy move. It doesn't matter what you do; the important thing is that you try something new from time to time. You may inspire him to return the favour!

## $Spice$ $It$ $Up$

- ☑ Serve him dessert in an apron . . . and nothing else.
- ☑ Put a special note in his fortune cookie or under his slice of cake.
- ☑ Challenge him to a game of strip poker.
- ☑ Give him a long, lingering sponge bath or joins him in the shower.
- ☑ Strip-tease him.
- ☑ Leave a thank-you note for the previous evening in his briefcase.
- ☑ Place goodies from the local sex shop in the medicine cabinet or night table. Waits for him to bring them up.
- ☑ Get fresh at the breakfast table.

# ROOM FOR IMPROVEMENT

There is no such thing as the perfect man. Sadly, this is an undisputable fact of life. Even your 'Mr. Right' could be 'Mr. Even Better'. Think of him as a work in progress. With a little spit and polish, and a little smoothing of the rough edges, your man could become a prize jewel instead of a rough diamond. There is always room for improvement.

## *Improving The Husband*

### Shopping

☑ A savvy woman knows that before she shops with her husband, she has to know her husband. Pay attention to what he normally tends to wear.

☑ Men are creatures of habit. If he's been comfortable wearing the same brand of jeans or shirts for years, it's going to take some time to bring him around to the idea of a suit. Be patient, focus on baby steps and be encouraged by any progress, no matter how small.

### Health

☑ Incorporate exercise into your daily life together. Take regular walks after dinner, make gym dates, and take your bikes with you on holiday.

☑ Keep him on a balanced diet and make sure he drinks in moderation.

☑ Stock the fridge full of healthy foods to ease him out of his poor habits. Using low-fat versions of cream cheese, butter and oil hopefully won't even register with him.

## Chivalry

 Teaching manners to a grown man is akin to teaching a horse to count, but it is not impossible. If you kindly remind him when he offends your sensibilities or embarrasses you, he'll soon learn to modify his behaviour accordingly.

 Be honest and direct. If he fails to hold doors open for you, take matters into your own hands. Before the door swings back into your face, ask him to open the door for you as you approach it.

If you are walking down the street, ask him to walk next to the curb. If you continually ask him to display good manners in a considerate way, he will naturally incorporate more gentlemanly behaviour.

## Culture

 Don't be complacent in seeking out new experiences – getting him to take an interest in cultural pursuits is not as difficult as it may seem.

 Pair the activity with his interests. For instance, if he is a sports buff, take him to a book signing for the latest best-selling sports biography.

 Enroll in classes together. Wine-tasting is a popular choice for men, concerned as it is with the consumption of alcohol.

 If you enjoy going out to dinner, take turns picking out restaurants to sample.

 Ease him into the theatre. Start with comedies and as he becomes more enthusiastic, try dramas or musicals.

 Gallery openings are a great way to get him into an artistic forum. There is usually food and drink, and lots of interesting people, so even if he isn't interested in the art, there is still something for him to do.

# 3

# SETTING UP HOME

They say 'home is where the heart is'. It follows then, that finding a new home that is perfect for you, and looking after it, will do wonders for your heart. If you are careful about choosing a new home, decorating it and maintaining it, there will certainly be beneficial effects for your happiness and well-being.

# THE NEW NEST

After choosing the man you want to live with, choosing a home to live in together is the most important decision you can make. Sadly, even as a Domestic Goddess, this is not a decision you can make alone. If it was, the whole process would be quick and easy, but unfortunately, you really will have to allow The Husband man to be part of the decision-making, so that your new home feels like it belongs to you both. I know. It is going to hurt. His aesthetic appreciation of pebble-dashing and avocado bathroom suites is going to slow you down somewhat. But grit your teeth and hang on in there.

## WORKING TOGETHER

Hunting for your new love nest requires a great deal of diplomacy and compromise, especially if you are going to navigate your way around his questionable taste. It is as well for the two of you to draw up a list of criteria, ranked in importance. Mark the things you would like in a house – the qualities that you consider desirable but not essential, those that you really couldn't live without, and those that, quite simply, you are not prepared to compromise on. Your priorities will reveal much about each other.

Of course location and finances will have a huge bearing on the kind of house you are looking for. When you add these considerations to the equation, choosing your new home together is fraught with potential difficulties. You will both have to do some serious compromising. Do you really have to live on the same road as your mother? Do you really need a huge garden/extra bedroom/whirlpool bath?

Remember, this should be a time of great excitement and adventure. You are starting a new life together and your new home is symbolic of the commitment you have made to each other. Don't rush into anything – take your time and consider every angle.

# ROOM TO BREATHE

While it may be tempting to spend all your time together when you're in the throes of brand-new cohabitation, remember to play it cool. You don't want to smother one another. And if The Husband has had commitment issues in the past (and what man hasn't?), his head may already be spinning at the thought of his bachelor life ending for good. He might miss his time alone or his time with the boys. If every time he turns around he sees you there, this panic will escalate. So remember the lessons you learned while dating: leave him wanting more.

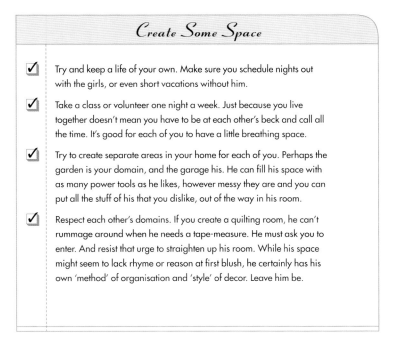

## Create Some Space

☑   Try and keep a life of your own. Make sure you schedule nights out with the girls, or even short vacations without him.

☑   Take a class or volunteer one night a week. Just because you live together doesn't mean you have to be at each other's beck and call all the time. It's good for each of you to have a little breathing space.

☑   Try to create separate areas in your home for each of you. Perhaps the garden is your domain, and the garage his. He can fill his space with as many power tools as he likes, however messy they are and you can put all the stuff of his that you dislike, out of the way in his room.

☑   Respect each other's domains. If you create a quilting room, he can't rummage around when he needs a tape-measure. He must ask you to enter. And resist that urge to straighten up his room. While his space might seem to lack rhyme or reason at first blush, he certainly has his own 'method' of organisation and 'style' of decor. Leave him be.

# CITY OR COUNTRY

Unless it's a foregone conclusion that your new nest will be in a particular location, this is something you need to discuss as a couple. If one of you is a 'city mouse' and the other a 'country mouse', perhaps you can agree on something in between – such as a peaceful suburb with an easy commute to town. If he loves the urban environment and you long for a rustic country retreat near a lake, be creative. Could you live in the city and put money aside for a weekend place? Could living more cheaply in the suburbs or countryside allow for a weekend per month at a fancy hotel in the city? Or could you agree on a timeline that suits your lifestyle – say the next few years in the city, followed by a move to somewhere quieter when you're ready to start a family?

## The City

| | Pros | | Cons |
|---|---|---|---|
| ✓ | Diversity of experiences and people | ✗ | Expense (including insurance and other hidden costs) |
| ✓ | Entertainment and cultural events | ✗ | Crime |
| ✓ | Restaurants and bars | ✗ | Litter |
| ✓ | Sense of fun and excitement | ✗ | Less family-friendly |
| ✓ | Public transport, easily walkable | ✗ | Limited space |
| ✓ | Historical points of interest | ✗ | Noise |
| | | ✗ | Few green spots |

## The Suburbs

| | Pros | | Cons |
|---|---|---|---|
| ✓ | Less expensive | ✗ | Can be bland and dull |
| ✓ | Quiet and serene | ✗ | Feeling of isolation |
| ✓ | Safe | ✗ | Less diversity, vibrancy |
| ✓ | Sense of community | ✗ | Family-oriented (only a con if you don't have kids) |
| ✓ | Ease of lifestyle | ✗ | More drive time |
| ✓ | Clean, new housing | ✗ | Fewer cultural or historical points of interest |
| ✓ | Spacious | | |

# IDEAL BEDROOM

If you've been living on your own for a long while, it may be a shock to have a man in your bedroom every night and every morning. It may also have obvious advantages. It can take some getting used to the piles of clothes he leaves at the foot of the bed or the gym shoes or the sports magazines stacked on the bedside table, the truth is the bedroom now belongs to both of you – and it should feel like it. Fill the bedroom with the colours and smells you both enjoy; keep electronics and work items out of sight; and use the bedroom for only two things: sleeping and lovemaking. By treating the bedroom as a romantic retreat for the two of you at the end of the day, you'll start to see him regard it this way too.

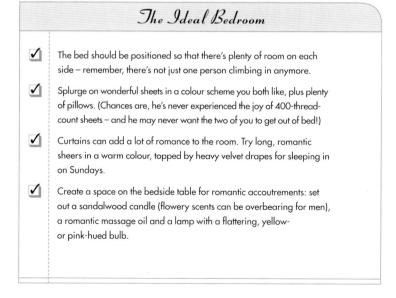

### The Ideal Bedroom

✓ The bed should be positioned so that there's plenty of room on each side – remember, there's not just one person climbing in anymore.

✓ Splurge on wonderful sheets in a colour scheme you both like, plus plenty of pillows. (Chances are, he's never experienced the joy of 400-thread-count sheets – and he may never want the two of you to get out of bed!)

✓ Curtains can add a lot of romance to the room. Try long, romantic sheers in a warm colour, topped by heavy velvet drapes for sleeping in on Sundays.

✓ Create a space on the bedside table for romantic accoutrements: set out a sandalwood candle (flowery scents can be overbearing for men), a romantic massage oil and a lamp with a flattering, yellow- or pink-hued bulb.

☑ Try to restrain yourself from filling your bedroom with florals and frillies – too many flowers and girly touches can make a man feel quite uncomfortable. Also remember that you are a little old for cuddly toys now. Say goodbye and put them away. You're a big girl now.

☑ Stock your favourite sensual aids in your bedside table so they're close at hand.

☑ Keep plenty of sexy CDs in the bedroom: Try jazz, or easy-listening chillout music.

☑ If you must keep office items in this room, store them in a cupboard or closed box.

☑ Keep the walls of your room pale. You can easily add colour and personalise your space by selecting pictures and adding soft furnishings to your tastes – and these things are easy to change as time goes by.

☑ No work. Period. Bringing work into the bedroom adds a stressful element to what should be an enjoyable, sensual and peaceful environment. If you need a comfortable place to go through your paperwork or to work on your laptop, try the sofa!

☑ Keep a laundry basket in the corner so you're not distracted during love-making by an unsightly heap of dirty clothes on the floor. It will also make it easy for The Husband to keep things tidy if there's a receptacle close at hand for his clothes at the end of each day.

# PETS

Owning a dog or a cat – or even a goldfish – can bring a new dimension to your home and your relationship. They can give you a sense of shared commitment – without going the whole hog and creating babies together!

## CHOOSING A PET

Pets are a serious responsibility though – almost as much as having children – and require constant care, training and attention. If you decide to add a pet to your happy home, you must put a great deal of thought into whether you actually have the space, time and money to look after one. Don't rush out and buy the cutest puppy you see without checking the breed out first – you

need to consider important details such as, exactly how big is that cute little puppy going to end up?

Think about the type of animal you want to have and what time and effort you are prepared to spend on it. You must also consider the practicalities of making arrangements for your pet to be looked after when you go away on holiday or just want to take a weekend break. Spontaneity is somewhat curtailed when you have a pet to consider. If dogs are too high-maintenance for you, and cats make you sneeze, fish always make excellent pets, and they require very little care. They also look gorgeous and can be used to great decorative effect to brighten up a dreary kitchen or bathroom!

## House Rules For Pets

☑ It's a good idea to establish some house rules, such as where your pet will be sleeping, if he is allowed to sit on the sofa, and who's taking him for walkies.

☑ Start as you mean to go on – if you have decided that your dog or cat is not allowed upstairs on the beds, don't cave in when you bring him home for his first night. Set his basket down in an out of the way place where Fido will feel relatively undisturbed.

☑ Use child safety gates to enforce the boundaries inside your house until your dog has learnt where he can and cannot go. It is a lot like training The Husband – set the ground rules and don't deviate from them.

# STORAGE

Adequate storage is absolutely imperative if you are not to live in chaos. Finding a place for everything requires just a little thought. Put spare linen in old drawers and then add castors and slide them under the bed. Run up a few simple drawstring bags and hang them on the back of doors for storing scarves, toys, potatoes, shoe-cleaning equipment. Make unusual shelving with distressed old floorboards propped up on house-bricks for all your novels. Get hold of those big storage bags that use the nozzle of the vacuum cleaner into to draw out the air. It makes storing bulky items such as spare duvets and winter coats much more space-saving, as they will slide, neatly, under the bed or on top of the wardrobe. There are no hard and fast rules about storage, so you can be as creative or as predictable as you like – just make sure you have plenty.

## A WORD ON BASKETS

You can't have too many baskets, they are one of the most effective weapons in a Domestic Goddess's household armoury. They are available in all shapes and sizes and can be used in every room of the house. Put them in bathrooms for cosmetics and bottles, on the hall table for letters and bills, in the sitting room for discarded newspapers – you get the idea.

You can tidy a room in no time at all, if you just bundle it all into a basket, and once a week you can sort out the contents and return things to their rightful place. The paperwork in your office can be stored in baskets. The vegetables in your kitchen can live in baskets hung from the ceiling. The children's toys are sorted into baskets. Stack newspapers and magazines into a basket in the sitting room. When you have finished opening the post, toss it in to – yes, you've guessed it – a basket. At the risk of repeating myself, you just can't have too many baskets.

# TASKS FOR EVERYDAY

Being prepared is half the battle. This means having the right equipment for the right job. It makes things a lot easier if you keep a set of cleaning tools in a cupboard on each floor of your house so you don't waste time running up and down the stairs. (Although, if you are a little disorganised, comfort yourself with the thought that the extra effort required in locating where you left the furniture polish is burning calories.) Fill a container with the cleaning materials that you use most often and a few bin liners. When you set out to clean, just reach into the cupboard, grab the bucket and go. Everything you need is in one place.

## ESTABLISH A SYSTEM

Some women prefer to work to a schedule. However, it is too easy to become disappointed and feel like a failure when you can't stick to it. And let's face it, life does have a funny habit of getting in the way of things like cleaning out the fridge or dusting behind the book shelf. So it makes sense to prioritise household chores into everyday essential jobs and those that only need to be done now and again. When the to-do list is shorter, and the end in sight, the housework will instantly feel more manageable.

You need to know that if anyone drops by, you can throw open her front door and welcome them in – without dying of mortification because the kitchen looks like a bomb has exploded, there are kids' toys all over the floor and the downstairs lavatory smells like a public convenience. What you need is a system – not a schedule – which basically means all communal areas get a swift 'going over' every day. If you get into the habit of tidying a room as you leave, it will be a lot more manageable. Imagine your mother-in-law might appear unannounced on your doorstep at any minute, that should encourage you to keep everything in order.

## DAILY MAINTENANCE

There are certain essential tasks which you should try to do everyday. Done regularly, they shouldn't take long – it's only when you've let your clothes pile up in a heap on the floor all week that sorting them out becomes a chore.

---

### *Everyday Tasks*

☑ Get into the habit of wiping over your kitchen surfaces after you have prepared food or made a cup of tea, so that they always look clean and tidy.

☑ Load dirty dishes straight into the dishwasher after meals and stack things to be washed by hand neatly beside the sink. If you clear up as you go, your kitchen will never be an embarrassment.

☑ Bathrooms need only brief attention on a daily basis – just ensure towels are hung up and dirty clothes are actually in the laundry basket, tidy toothbrushes and cosmetics, run a cloth over the sink and check the toilet bowl is clean.

☑ Fold your clothes before you climb into bed at night, or throw them into the laundry basket. Remember, you are much less likely to feel in a seductive mood if you have to negotiate your way past piles of dirty laundry to get to the bed.

☑ Always make the bed in the morning. You needn't think hospital bed corners every day, especially if you're in a rush. Just straightening out the sheets and pillows, instead of a crumpled mess, will make a difference to the room.

☑ Straighten out all the surfaces in the bedroom, including your dressing table, and open up the windows (remember to shut them again if you're leaving the house). It is highly unlikely that you will be receiving visitors in your bedroom but it is so much more restful to

---

retire to a tidy room at night. At least try to make an effort to keep it tidy and fresh.

☑ Always keep the hallway in order – it is the first thing your mother-in-law will see. Tidy the table and wipe the mirror. Run the vacuum cleaner around if necessary. A bunch of fresh flowers in a prominent position works wonders.

☑ Hang up all hats and coats, preferably out of the way in a downstairs cupboard if possible.

☑ If you plump up the cushions, tidy the surfaces and straighten the rug in the sitting room before you go to bed every night, you will only have to vacuum and flick a duster around a couple of times a week.

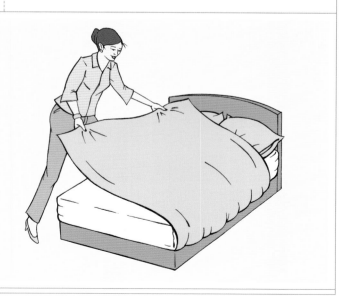

# TASKS FOR A RAINY DAY

There are certain household chores that you can leave for a more convenient time without having to worry about your status as a Domestic Goddess. No one will know how long it's been since you last cleared the guttering after all. Just bear in mind that they will have to be done one day.

*Rainy Day Tasks*

✓ It makes sense to have a bi-annual clearout of your wardrobe. As the autumn approaches, it is a good idea to sort through your clothes and put away the things you won't wear again until next spring.

✓ Make sure you wash or dry clean everything you store, adding some cedar chippings or lavender bags to ward off the moths. Fix broken zips, loose seams and unravelling hems, and put everything away in the loft or under the spare room bed.

✓ Offer to have a seasonal sort-out of your husband's wardrobe too. This is the perfect time to 'lose' questionable items like that hideous Christmas jumper from his great aunt, with the reindeer on the front. By the time next winter comes around and he gets his woolies out of storage, he'll have forgotten all about them.

✓ Defrost the freezer quarterly as it makes it far more efficient to run, as well as giving you more space inside.

✓ Clear the guttering. Technically you could do this yourself, but why bother? Leave it to The Husband, unless you have a gardener or handyman. Remind him to get out the step-ladder and clear the guttering of accumulated leaves and debris before autumn and again in the spring, to prevent blockages and potential flood disasters!

# DECORATIVE TOUCHES

This is one area where your opinion may clash with The Husband's. It is worth remembering that compared to your exquisite tastes, men really don't have the aesthetic sensitivity to judge what is decorative and what is not. Don't doubt your own taste and under no circumstances should you listen to anything he has to say on the subject of soft-furnishings.

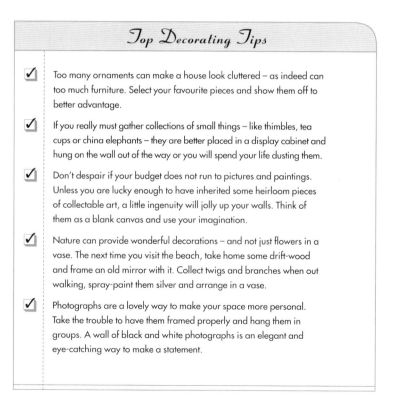

## Top Decorating Tips

☑ Too many ornaments can make a house look cluttered – as indeed can too much furniture. Select your favourite pieces and show them off to better advantage.

☑ If you really must gather collections of small things – like thimbles, tea cups or china elephants – they are better placed in a display cabinet and hung on the wall out of the way or you will spend your life dusting them.

☑ Don't despair if your budget does not run to pictures and paintings. Unless you are lucky enough to have inherited some heirloom pieces of collectable art, a little ingenuity will jolly up your walls. Think of them as a blank canvas and use your imagination.

☑ Nature can provide wonderful decorations – and not just flowers in a vase. The next time you visit the beach, take home some drift-wood and frame an old mirror with it. Collect twigs and branches when out walking, spray-paint them silver and arrange in a vase.

☑ Photographs are a lovely way to make your space more personal. Take the trouble to have them framed properly and hang them in groups. A wall of black and white photographs is an elegant and eye-catching way to make a statement.

# 4

# MAINTAINING THE HOME

A bit like having a tooth pulled or paying your taxes, cleaning and repairs are among life's little duties that just cannot be avoided. It is better not to fight it, just accept the inevitable, take a deep breath and get on with it. Keep in mind that it is hard to live in domestic bliss if you're constantly navigating piles of laundry and dirty dishes. They won't clean themselves, and relying on The Husband to do it isn't recommended. You'll just have to get your hands dirty every now and then.

# TIPS FOR SAVING TIME

A Domestic Goddess is an efficient housekeeper. You need to know not just how to clean well, but how to clean quickly – get it over and done with so that you have plenty of time to get on with the more important things in life. Of course, an easy way to save time is knowing when to delegate – in certain cases it is possible to train The Husband to locate the on/off switch of the vacuum cleaner and even to apply cleaning fluid to the bathroom tiles (This is made infinitely easier if you buy cleanser that comes with a spray nozzle. Use words like 'aim', 'trigger' and 'fire' and you may find he catches on more quickly). As a general rule of thumb though, it is usually much safer and more efficient to tackle certain jobs oneself – particularly those that require a basic understanding of hygiene. Having established a cleaning system and created some ingenious storage solutions, your home will now run like clockwork. But there are a few more useful tips to have up your sleeve . . .

## Top Time-Saving Tips

- ☑ Don't make hard work out of cleaning the lavatory. Pour in some bleach before you go to bed once or twice a week. A good soaking means that deposits are not allowed to build up.

- ☑ Fold a complete set of bed linen (duvet cover and sheet) into the matching pillowcase, so that it is all together neatly in one bundle.

- ☑ An adhesive roller for removing lint is handy for all sorts of jobs, making light work of removing large amounts of pet hair from Rover's favourite chair or the back of your car, or your Afghan rug.

- ☑ A little furniture polish, sprayed onto skirting boards and door frames, acts as a dust-repellent.

Save your left-over lemons and use them to clean the microwave. Just pop in a few spent halves, switch on to full power for 30 seconds and the naturally acidic lemon oils distribute themselves over the interior of the oven, meaning you can remove grease and grime with just a quick wipe of a cloth.

 The quickest and most efficient way to clean windows and mirrors is with good old-fashioned vinegar and newspaper. It leaves the surface smear- and streak-free and takes no time at all.

 Use baking soda to clean the fridge – it is very efficient and eliminates odours.

 Use old plastic carrier bags to line waste bins in the bedrooms and bathrooms, and keep some spares in each room. It makes emptying them much quicker as you can just lift out the bag, tie up the handles and deposit in the rubbish.

 Finally, keep all the equipment you need as close to the place where you are going to use it as possible. It makes things a lot easier if you keep a set of cleaning tools in a cupboard on each floor of your house so you don't waste time running up and down the stairs.

# SPRING CLEAN

Traditionally the house was given a thorough 'Spring Cleaning' but it doesn't particularly matter at what time of the year you choose to have a cleaning blitz, as long as you do try and get it done once a year.

## CARPETS AND SOFT FURNISHINGS

Carpets require an annual deep-clean – you can hire carpet-cleaning equipment quite cheaply and do it yourself, or if that sounds a bit ambitious, you can get the professionals in to do it for you.

Take down your curtains once a year and remove the loose covers on sofas and armchairs. If you are able to machine-wash everything, so much the better, but it may be that a trip to the dry-cleaners is in order. A thorough cleaning gives them a whole new lease of life.

## WALLS AND WOODWORK

A gentle circular rubbing with a soft damp cloth and some kitchen cleanser should eradicate dirty marks on light coloured paint but watch out for coloured wallpaper if you are using a particularly astringent cleaning fluid. Even more effective is a child's pencil eraser. This will all become a more regular part of your household maintenance routine when your children arrive as little fingers leave grubby handprints on your magnolia emulsion.

## PROFESSIONAL CLEANERS

If you can afford to do it, you might consider hiring the professionals to 'spring clean' your house for you. You could arrange for it to coincide with your annual holiday or a weekend away. Being a Domestic Goddess is about knowing when to cut corners and which corners to cut.

# DIY

While a you may be well aware that DIY stands for 'Do It Yourself', you may want to take a more flexible approach to the 'Yourself' part of doing it. There are some jobs which are always better delegated. However, you should always be properly prepared for minor DIY tasks and know exactly what essential tools you must keep to hand for such eventualities.

## Toolkit Essentials

- ✓ a selection of screwdrivers – both flat and cross-head
- ✓ a small hacksaw
- ✓ a utility knife – also called a box-cutter or Stanley knife
- ✓ a tape measure

- ✓ a claw hammer
- ✓ a drill
- ✓ a pair of pliers
- ✓ an adjustable spanner
- ✓ an assortment of nails, screws and rawlplugs

A word of warning when assembling your tool kit. Under no circumstances should you take The Husband with you. Men come over all unnecessary in these stores. If you allow him to decide what constitutes 'essential tools' you will end up having to remortgage your house to pay for an obscure, and positively dangerous, array of power tools. Imagine being let loose in a shoe shop – it is much the same thing. Leave him at home.

## PAINTING AND DECORATING

If you intend to tackle the decorating yourself, or even to project-manage the task, well done you. You will need to be organised and think things through though to make sure it all goes according to plan.

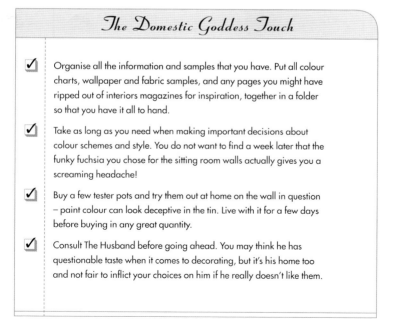

### The Domestic Goddess Touch

☑ Organise all the information and samples that you have. Put all colour charts, wallpaper and fabric samples, and any pages you might have ripped out of interiors magazines for inspiration, together in a folder so that you have it all to hand.

☑ Take as long as you need when making important decisions about colour schemes and style. You do not want to find a week later that the funky fuchsia you chose for the sitting room walls actually gives you a screaming headache!

☑ Buy a few tester pots and try them out at home on the wall in question – paint colour can look deceptive in the tin. Live with it for a few days before buying in any great quantity.

☑ Consult The Husband before going ahead. You may think he has questionable taste when it comes to decorating, but it's his home too and not fair to inflict your choices on him if he really doesn't like them.

# FABRIC CARE FOR BEGINNERS

Understanding fabric care labels is essential to the maintenance of your clothes and other washable items. To avoid washday disasters it is important to read the manufacturer's laundry instructions and to follow them. Otherwise you run the risk of shrinkage, non-fast colours running, bobbling, puckering, rips or worse . . .

## Rules for Laundry Day

☑ Don't be frightened. Although it sounds as if you are navigating your washing through a minefield, care instructions are easy to follow when you understand the basics and the symbols.

☑ Sort your laundry into four separate piles – whites, lights, coloureds and handwash.

☑ Empty all pockets – items such as bank notes and passports are not improved by a run through the wash.

☑ Do up zips, hooks and fasteners that might snag other clothing or work loose.

☑ It is a good idea to soak or pre-treat heavily soiled items before washing, or you can end up redistributing dirt onto less soiled items in the machine.

☑ Check the label to see what each garment is made of. The fabric content should be clearly visible and this is your first clue to the appropriate care. Cottons can generally withstand higher temperatures, but synthetics need a cooler wash. Be careful with natural linens as they can easily shrink.

✓ Some things are better washed inside out – particularly clothing with transfers or embroidery – but jeans will fade less quickly too if you turn them the wrong way round. The care label on the garment should indicate if it needs to be washed inside out.

✓ Check the recommended temperature for each garment and use the lowest setting for the whole load.

✓ Try and wash items of a similar weight together – delicates fare better washed separately from heavier fabrics.

✓ Don't be tempted to overfill the machine – clothes need enough space to be agitated correctly to facilitate the washing process.

✓ Use a mesh bag to wash fragile lingerie and refrain from putting underwired bras in the machine. The wires are prone to coming loose and can bend, snag other clothing or, worse, get lodged in the drum of your machine.

✓ Don't leave your laundry in the machine for long periods of time once the wash cycle is complete. Try to hang it up, or put it in the dryer straight away.

| Drying | Do not bleach | Hand-wash only |
|---|---|---|

| Do not tumble-dry | Do not iron | Dry-clean only |
|---|---|---|

# IRONING

Housewives generally fall into two camps when it comes to ironing. They either find it mind-numbingly boring and largely unnecessary, or strangely soothing and therapeutic. Women, and some men, who fall into the latter category are the type who tend to iron their underpants.

If your opinion of ironing is mostly of the first attitude, do not worry. It is quite normal, dare I say healthy, to pay it scant regard. There are a few things you can do to lessen the pain.

## *Easy Ironing*

☑ Set up your ironing board in front of the TV or put the radio on.

☑ Divide your ironing into bundles of three items and reward yourself with a chocolate truffle every time you complete a pile.

☑ Heavy trousers, cords or jeans, can be shaken from the washing machine and straightened by hand while still damp, then stretched over the back of a chair or hung over a door overnight to dry.

☑ Never let anything sit in the tumble dryer after it has finished. If you take everything out when it is still warm and fold it up neatly, most things will not need ironing. Hang shirts straight onto hangers, leave to air and you'll be surprised how little pressing they actually require.

☑ Cheat when ironing bed linen – don't bother with the under-sheet at all and only press the side of the pillowcase and duvet cover that can be seen.

☑ It is a good idea to avoid ironing anything delicate at all, particularly if it is an expensive or precious item of clothing. Use a professional cleaning service.

☑ Life is far too short to spend one precious moment ironing underwear or socks.

☑ To reduce the amount you have to iron, try investing in some non-iron or crease-resistant clothing. The odd blouse or shirt to wear to work wouldn't hurt and might prove useful on those mornings when you have overslept.

☑ If you are lucky enough to have an Aga or a large range cooker, you can fold slightly damp cottons on to the closed lids of the hot plates – particularly tea-towels and pillowcases – and not a jot of ironing will be necessary.

# STAIN REMOVAL

Whoops. You've spilt red wine on the carpet. Yes, even a Domestic Goddess has occasional unavoidable accidents, but as long as you know exactly what to do about them, disaster can be averted. The golden rule with stains is not to hang about but to treat them immediately, whether on clothing, carpets, upholstery or floors. The longer you leave it the harder it is to get the stain out.

## IMMEDIATE ACTION

Firstly, move all animals, children and husbands away from the disaster area and out of your way. They might be tempted to help. If need be, send them away to fetch a cloth. Then you will need to scrape up any excess surface matter before you start the stain removal process, and attempt to blot as much of the stain away as you can. Notice I say blot – not rub. The idea is to absorb as much of the stain away as possible rather than spread it about. For the same reason, always work from the outside of the stain in.

Be exceedingly careful if you are using homemade remedies on stains and marks. For instance, throwing white wine or salt on top of a red wine stain might dilute the colouring, but it can also damage delicate fabric. Don't use hot water if you are not sure what the stain is, and always use a proper stain remover designed for the job wherever possible.

Of course if you don't have a proper one to hand you still need to be able to do something about the stain quickly, and there are some tried and tested methods for removing stubborn stains which can be surprisingly effective. They also have the added bonus of not requiring the use of strong or harmful chemicals and are thus much kinder to the environment.

Always remember to be patient when tackling stains. Stain removal is not an exact science, so don't expect instant miracles – the cleaning solution will take time to be effective.

### *Emergency First Aid For Stains*

| | |
|---|---|
| Blood | Soak the stain immediately in cold water – never hot water as that will set the stain. Toothpaste and milk have also been known to work. |
| Candle wax | Leave the wax to solidify and then gently scrape as much as you can off with a blunt flat-edged knife. Lay a sheet of grease-proof paper over (and if possible under) the mark and dry-iron on the lowest temperature. This works on carpets and fabrics. |
| Chewing gum | Place the item in the freezer and allow the gum to harden, and it should come off easily. Then wash according to the label. This also works for chocolate. |
| Red or white wine | Ignore the old wives' tales about throwing salt or more wine of either colour at it. Soak in soda water immediately. Follow by the hottest wash possible according to the care label. This also works for tea and coffee stains. |
| Ballpoint pen | Try dabbing with neat methylated spirits on a cotton wool pad, then wash as normal or rub the stain gently using a pencil eraser to fade the mark. |
| | *continued on next page* |

| | *continued* |
|---|---|
| Cooking oil or fat | Sprinkle talcum powder over the stain. Leave for 30 minutes and brush off. Wash as normal. |
| Mildew | First, take the item outside and remove the surface mildew with a stiff brush. Leave to air out in the sun. If spots remain, wash in biological detergent. |
| Rust | Douse the stain with salt, then pour lemon juice over and put the garment outside in the sun. A small mark should fade after a few hours, a heavier mark may take days. |
| Mud | Allow the mud to dry, brush off, soak in cool water and wash as normal. Some women used to swear by rubbing dried-on mud with a raw potato. |
| Perspiration | Sponge underarm perspiration with white wine vinegar, rinse then wash as usual. |

## DOS AND DON'TS

| | |
|---|---|
| [X] | Do not try to remove stains on silk by rubbing, you'll break fibres and end up with a lighter area that can't be removed. |
| [X] | Do not treat a dry-clean only garment with a water-based stain remover. You'll be left with a watermark. |
| [X] | If a precious or irreplaceable fabric has been soiled, it is absolutely imperative that you do not attempt to treat the stain at home. Leave it to the professionals. Take it as soon as possible to a specialist cleaner. |

# SEWING TIPS AND PROJECTS FOR BEGINNERS

When a button drops off The Husband's shirt or the hem comes loose on your favourite dress, don't panic. All you need to do is whip out your needle and set to work with the confidence of a professional seamstress. Now, if bias-binding sounds like one-sided bondage and you thought basting was something one does to a turkey, don't panic. Minor clothing repairs are easy when you know how. First you will need a basic sewing kit.

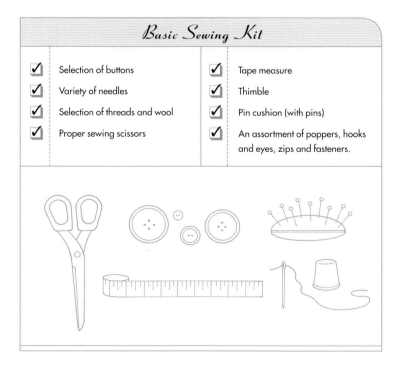

## Basic Sewing Kit

- ✓ Selection of buttons
- ✓ Variety of needles
- ✓ Selection of threads and wool
- ✓ Proper sewing scissors

- ✓ Tape measure
- ✓ Thimble
- ✓ Pin cushion (with pins)
- ✓ An assortment of poppers, hooks and eyes, zips and fasteners.

## MENDING PROJECTS

Now you have got your basic sewing kit organised, you are ready to tackle those minor clothing repairs.

### Replace A Button

| *You will need* | **H O W  T O . . .** |
|---|---|
| **needle** | **1** Thread your needle and knot the end. |
| **thread (a close colour match to the button)** | **2** Make a small stitch in the right side of the fabric where the button will sit and pull through to the knot. Do this again once or twice, so you have a firm base to work from. |
| **a spare button** | **3** Insert the needle through one of the holes in the back of the button, and thread it along until it is on the fabric at the right spot. |
| | **4** Following the stitch pattern of the other buttons, pass your needle across the front of the button and down through another hole making a very small stitch in the fabric behind. Repeat this process four or five times until the button feels secure. |
| | **5** To finish off, make a small stitch in the fabric and then wind the thread tightly, several times, around the stitches you have made behind the button. Then insert the needle through the stitches and pull through only partially to form a loop. Insert your needle through the loop and pull tight. Repeat. |

## Sew Up A Loose Hem

### You will need

**an iron**

**needle**

**thread (a close colour match to the fabric)**

**pins**

### HOW TO...

**1** Give the hem a good pressing with an iron. This will help to hold it in shape.

**2** Secure the fabric with pins – try and place them half way between the top and the bottom of the hem, so that you do not have to remove the pins while you sew.

**3** Thread your needle and knot the end.

**4** Try to replicate the stitch pattern of the garment as closely as possible. Start about 2 cm (0.8 in) away from the loose area, so that your first stitches are reinforcing the existing stitching.

**5** Secure your thread by making a very small stitch in the hem, not the skirt. Pull through to the knot and repeat. Then bring your needle to the skirt, using the tiniest stitches you can, picking up just one or two fibres of the fabric, so that from the right side they will be invisible. Pass the needle back through the hem.

**6** Move along the skirt 1 cm (0.4 in) and repeat, until you have covered the area that was loose. Finish about 2 cm (0.8 in) past the loose area.

**7** Finish by making a last stitch and passing the needle through the loop, as with the button.

# TIME TO CALL FOR HELP

Looking after the technology that fills the modern home requires a little extra care. There are times when even a Domestic Goddess will need some back-up around the home, even if it's just for a job you don't feel like doing. It is perfectly acceptable to call for help for any job you don't want to do, particularly if it is messy or time-consuming, as well as for those you can't handle yourself. Part of your extensive household management skills is knowing just when to call for help – and also knowing exactly whom to call.

## TACKLING TECHNOLOGY

When anything remotely expensive stops working in your house, it is time to call for help. Don't attempt to mend it yourself – it is absolutely not worth it, even if you are convinced you know what you are doing. Stop. Walk away. Pick up the phone. Get the professionals in. Machines such as computers and TV sets fall into this category, as do large kitchen appliances like cookers and fridges. Motor vehicles of any description, heating systems, hot water boilers and security alarms should all be added to the list. This is not a gender-related issue by any means – it is just a matter of being sensible. Think how irritated you will be if you have to replace the item because your attempts at fixing the problem actually broke it beyond repair. Don't fiddle.

If something sounds or looks complicated, it probably is complicated. It may not be a life-threatening task, but obviously if a job requires a level of knowledge or expertise that you just can't get from reading a 'How To' manual, it is sensible to find someone who knows what they are doing. Things like electrical or gas work, or substantial DIY projects that involve structural changes, should always be undertaken by a qualified professional. If ever in doubt on any of your machinery, call or drop in to an electrical store and ask for expert advice.

## *Living With Technology*

✓ Locate all technological equipment away from children so that they can't fiddle with moveable parts, press buttons, twiddle knobs or post things that don't belong into any slots.

✓ Always keep the instruction manuals that come with any new pieces of technolgy. The Husband may refuse to read it, but there may come a time when you need to work the machine yourself.

✓ Note down any serial numbers and helpline numbers for new machines in one place. Then when something does go wrong you know exactly where all the information is.

✓ Organise and tidy the unsightly jumbles of wires that proliferate around computers, printers, scanners, TVs, videos and DVD players with clever little cable clips.

✓ Label each electric plug so that you know which appliance it belongs to – especially useful if you are using four or even six socket extension adapters and you don't want to keep unplugging the wrong one.

✓ Keep your computer and printer in a separate office room if possible, or at least try not to have them in the bedroom. Your bedroom should be a place of sanctuary, not full of reminders of the stress of your job.

✓ Take control of your remote controls. Decide with where the remote is going to live and keep it there! Domestic harmony will follow.

# 5

# COOKING
# FOR
# EVERYDAY

With a little planning and preparation, cooking for everyday does not need to be a chore. Once you have equipped your kitchen properly, learnt how to plan your menus and shop sensibly, have a well-stocked store cupboard and a few quick meal ideas up your sleeve, you are well on your way to running the kitchen like a well-oiled machine. Like a Boy Scout, you need to be prepared.

# EQUIP YOUR KITCHEN

The most essential items to begin with are a fork and a corkscrew. There are lots and lots of things you can do with the fork, apart from eating: you can mash potatoes, whisk eggs, flip meat, and spear things. With the corkscrew, open the wine and pour yourself a glass. Then you're ready to start equipping your kitchen. There are certain pieces of kitchen equipment that you really just can't live without – without a tin opener you won't even be able to whip up beans on toast. Not without a fair amount of struggle anyway. There are other items that although certainly helpful, are not absolutely essential if you're not overly ambitious in the kitchen. (But of course as a Domestic Goddess, that doesn't apply to you). Technically a food processor is a non-essential item, but it is very useful for the tedious jobs like chopping large amounts of onion or making breadcrumbs.

## THE DINNER SERVICE

Choosing a dinner service is one of those monumental decisions that will have an impact on your life for many years to come. After choosing a man and a house, it is could be the next most important choice you will make. It won't be cheap but it should see you through a few decades of service. Much like a husband. Take your time deciding which china to opt for. Don't listen to The Husband. Men generally don't have a clue about appropriate tableware and so forth, and nor do they care. They would be just as happy eating off disposable paper plates.

Stick with the plain and simple for cutlery and glassware. To start with, just get four wine glasses and four hi-balls for everyday use. Cutlery needs to go in the dishwasher, so avoid silver for everyday use – you have plenty to do as it is without creating any more chores for yourself.

## Kitchen Essentials

- ☑ small sharp knife
- ☑ large saucepan (with lid)
- ☑ small saucepan
- ☑ frying pan
- ☑ large sieve
- ☑ roasting tray
- ☑ large sharp knife
- ☑ bread knife
- ☑ wooden spoon
- ☑ tin opener
- ☑ colander
- ☑ cheese grater
- ☑ stockpot

- ☑ casserole dish with lid
- ☑ rubber and wooden spatulas
- ☑ whisk
- ☑ kitchen scissors
- ☑ potato masher
- ☑ set of scales
- ☑ vegetable peeler
- ☑ steamer
- ☑ wok
- ☑ large and small mixing bowls
- ☑ one or two jugs in different sizes

# LARDER ESSENTIALS

A well-stocked store-cupboard is an essential part of an efficiently run home. If you always have the basics to hand, you can rustle up a delicious meal at the drop of a hat for unannounced visitors, or when you are short of time.

## Stocking Your Larder

✓ In addition to the fresh produce you buy regularly, keep a variety of dried food in the larder, such as pasta, rice and assorted dried fruits. Then you will never be caught short and will always have the means to put a good meal on the table. A selection of dried herbs is especially useful for emergencies.

✓ Don't turn your nose up at convenience food like canned goods. There are some excellent products available now in tins, such as a variety of canned beans and fruits, which have a long shelf life, and will always come in useful (tinned meat is never a good idea though).

✓ Try and remember to replace items after you use them, so that you always have them in stock for the next meal.

✓ Online shopping can make the nightmare of tackling supermarket shopping a quick and easy experience – with the added benefit of being able to do it sitting down, and without leaving the house.

✓ Don't let The Husband know just how quickly you can whip up a mouth-watering meal from your larder stocks. It should help to prevent him getting into the habit of bringing people home without due warning or throwing impromptu parties.

# MENU PLANNING

One of the easiest ways to stay on top in the kitchen, especially during a busy week, is to plan your meals for the week in advance. Before you do your weekly shop, write a list of all the meals you will serve that week. The trick is to plan your menus by combining ingredients, so that you do not waste time or money by buying things that will serve only for one meal.

A good place to start is with a joint of meat, which will perhaps be roasted for Sunday lunch – you'll feel like the ultimate Domestic Goddess serving up a traditional family feast. It is a false economy to buy a small joint – get a large one and it will stretch to several more meals. For instance, the left-over roast meat from a chicken could then be used to make a curry and a pasta dish, while the carcass can then be boiled up for stock to make sauces and soup.

Add a fair quantity of beef mince to your list and cook it up with some onions and garlic. Half of the mince mixture can be used for a cottage pie. Make a jug of gravy and a mountain of mashed potatoes and you can use some for the cottage pie and serve the rest another evening with sausages. The other half of the beef mince could be used for a chilli con carne.

## QUICK MEAL IDEAS

When planning your meals in advance, keep in mind that there will be some evenings when you simply won't have time to spend an hour preparing a meal, or two hours waiting for it to slow roast in the oven. You need to make sure you have some quick meal plans for such occasions.

Remember, fast food does not have to mean junk, unappetising, highly calorific and laden with fat. When you are short of time you can easily cook up some quick meals at home which look and taste great, and can even be good for you. Honestly.

## Quick Meals

☑ Pasta is the ultimate fast food. All you have to do is add some chopped ham or bacon, fresh tomatoes and grated cheese or try stirring through some pesto and creme fraiche and top with parmesan.

☑ Pan-fried steak needs little more on the plate than a fresh green salad and some buttery new potatoes. Add a dash of red wine to the pan and stir about to make the most of the meat juices for a quick gravy, or just let a wedge of blue cheese melt over the top.

☑ Slice a pocket in a chicken breast and pop in some sun dried tomatoes, a spoonful of pesto or cream cheese and wrap it all up in parma ham or bacon, and just leave it cooking while you have a well-earned rest.

☑ Chop some peppers and onions, spicy sausage and cooked potatoes, chuck into a pan and after five minutes pour over a couple of beaten eggs for a Spanish-style omelette.

☑ Fry some prawns or strips of beef with onions, garlic, ginger, peppers, broccoli, and noodles. Add soy sauce and a dash of sherry for a quick and tasty stir-fry.

☑ Jacket potatoes are fuss-free, even if they do take an hour in the oven – at least you can go and do something else while they are cooking. Then you can top with whatever you fancy, whether it's cheese, chilli con carne, or just a bit of butter.

# PREPARING MEALS IN ADVANCE

Life can be made so much easier when your meals are prepared in advance, and it's easy to do with a little forethought.

Of course your freezer will operate more efficiently if it is full, so keep it well-stocked. Just look at it as an extension of your larder – only colder – and it will become indispensable when planning and cooking in advance.

## *Planning Ahead*

☑ When you are peeling potatoes peel more than you need so that you can use them for tomorrow's meal as well.

☑ Roast the biggest chicken you can find and it will do three or four meals.

☑ Make double the quantity of casserole and freeze it.

☑ One of the easiest ways to plan ahead is to combine sensible shopping and menu planning with the use of a freezer.

☑ The freezer is extremely useful for catering in the event of life's little surprises – if unexpected guests appear, or if you are taken ill and The Husband must take over the cooking for a few days. Keep it well stocked for such eventualities.

☑ It is a good idea to check your freezer each week when you are writing up your menu plans to remind yourself what you have already got or what needs to be replaced.

☑ If you're freezing left overs, make sure you label the containers, with the date they go in, as well as what they are. Then you won't have to worry about just how long they may have been in there.

If you know you are going to need to take a meal out of the freezer in advance, write yourself a reminder to take it out in plenty of time for it to defrost.

 As well as storing uncooked meats, some fresh produce from your garden or a friend's allotment can be usefully frozen to enjoy out of season – especially handy if you have a glut.

 Keep a few luxury or gourmet ready meals in the freezer on stand by.

 Frozen vegetables are particularly convenient. One might even question the comparative nutritional goodness of a pea that has been preserved by freezing some hours after it was picked, with the 'fresh' pea that has travelled many thousands of miles to sit on a supermarket shelf for a few days.

# SNACKS AND TREATS

If The Husband feels hard done by while he is watching the ball game unless he is able to snack on something that comes out of a bag with his beer, you could get in some packets of pretzels or nuts, which are healthier than crisps or processed snacks. However, it is a lot more fun to make your own, which also means you can keep control of salt and fat content.

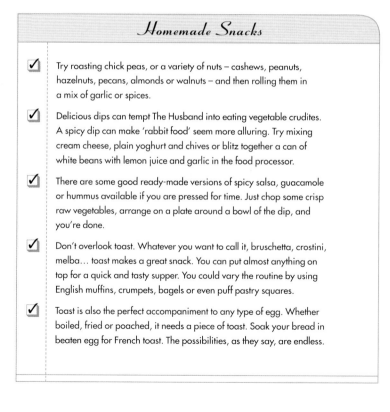

### *Homemade Snacks*

- ✓ Try roasting chick peas, or a variety of nuts – cashews, peanuts, hazelnuts, pecans, almonds or walnuts – and then rolling them in a mix of garlic or spices.

- ✓ Delicious dips can tempt The Husband into eating vegetable crudites. A spicy dip can make 'rabbit food' seem more alluring. Try mixing cream cheese, plain yoghurt and chives or blitz together a can of white beans with lemon juice and garlic in the food processor.

- ✓ There are some good ready-made versions of spicy salsa, guacamole or hummus available if you are pressed for time. Just chop some crisp raw vegetables, arrange on a plate around a bowl of the dip, and you're done.

- ✓ Don't overlook toast. Whatever you want to call it, bruschetta, crostini, melba… toast makes a great snack. You can put almost anything on top for a quick and tasty supper. You could vary the routine by using English muffins, crumpets, bagels or even puff pastry squares.

- ✓ Toast is also the perfect accompaniment to any type of egg. Whether boiled, fried or poached, it needs a piece of toast. Soak your bread in beaten egg for French toast. The possibilities, as they say, are endless.

# LOVE HIS FOOD

If you are a girl who likes her salads and lean meat, fresh seasonal produce and as few additives and E numbers as possible, you are going to find it difficult if he loves his junk food. There are many men who actually enjoy monosodium glutamate in all its glory (even a Domestic Goddess isn't always entirely immune to a sinful snack now and again).

## LEARN TO COMPROMISE

If you are sharing the responsibility of doing the cooking, when it is his turn ask that he gives you extra vegetables or some salad on the side. Suggest that he gets a take-away when you are out for the evening with friends. If he hates what you love, all is not lost. There are ways to work around the problem. Naturally, you can order your favourite foods when you are out with your girlfriends. If you don't eat red meat (or any kind of meat, for that matter), develop a few pasta dishes or casseroles where the meat is on the side or non-existent. He may be surprised how easy it is to forego meat. With careful planning, he may not even notice the omission at all! Swap spicy sausage for spinach in your lasagne and check his reaction, if he has one at all.

## MAKE HIS FAVOURITE DISHES

Pay attention to what he takes seconds of. When you are at a restaurant, notice what he tends to order. Does he love fish or is he a hard-core carnivore? Ask his mother what his favourite dishes from childhood are. Or take the next step and ask her to share the recipes with you. She'll love that and The Husband will love your meatloaf.

# 6

# HOSTING PARTIES

Being a perfect hostess comes naturally to a Domestic Goddess. Your parties are considered the social events of the year – people will queue round the block for an invitation to one of your shindigs. Your ability to throw a party for hundreds with consummate ease is legendary. She is always gracious, unruffled and hospitable. The secret to your social mastery is the same secret that makes you a Domestic Goddess. It is all in the preparation.

# BE PREPARED

As any girl guide will tell you, it pays to be prepared. No matter how well you've trained him, you never know when The Husband will bring home a colleague or his boss without giving you any warning. For moments such as these, it is worth making sure you have a few essentials in the house so that even when you're caught off guard you can still play the perfect hostess and have something to offer your guests.

## Meet and Greet

☑ Never make someone think they are unwelcome. When a guest shows up on your doorstep, always greet them with a smile even if they have caught you right in the middle of de-scaling the kettle or tidying The Husband's collection of ties.

☑ Make sure there are always a few bottles of wine in the cupboard and plenty of tea and coffee, so you can offer guests a welcome drink.

☑ Keep a box of luxury biscuits in the house for unexpected guests (remember to keep them hidden until you need them. Husbands and children have an annoying habit of being able to sniff out special treats at one hundred paces – a little like pigs rooting for truffles.)

☑ Keep one of your delicious homemade casseroles that you can defrost in the microwave in case they plan on staying for dinner.

☑ Even if you are only entertaining yourself and The Husband, eat your meals at the table. It will help encourage him to remember his table manners, and should a guest appear, you'll actually seem like a civilised, sophisticated couple enjoying an intimate dinner at the table.

# PERFECT HOSTESS

A perfect hostess always throws the perfect party, and all you need is a bit of planning – what food and drink to serve, how to create just the right atmosphere and ensure all your guests have the most marvellous time. Anyone can throw a good knees-up, but it is the attention to detail that elevates an ordinary party into a truly memorable occasion.

## BE MODERATELY MERRY!

Over-estimate the quantities you need – nothing kills a party stone-dead quite like running out of drink. You don't want people leaving early in search of a second glass! Make sure that you have plenty of soft drinks as well, for guests who are driving or who are inclined to be more sober.

Unless you are throwing a dinner party, it is a good idea to have some delicious nibbly things to offer your guests. Not only will people get hungry later in the evening, but there is the potential danger for wild drunkenness that accompanies drinking on an empty stomach. By all means cheat, and avail yourself of the wide variety of party food available ready-made at the supermarket. You will have enough to do, and these will just need heating up in the oven – a task you can safely delegate if necessary. And offering a tray of canapes around the room gives you the chance to mingle and chat with all of your guests.

## NEIGHBOURHOOD WATCH

Don't forget to invite your neighbours. Unless you are particularly friendly with them, it is unlikely they will come. However, if your party gets a little noisy – which can happen – they are forewarned and less likely to complain, as it would appear churlish.

## PUTTING YOUR GUESTS AT EASE

It is important to circulate around the room and chat with all those you have invited. Don't allow yourself to spend hours with only one or two of your friends, leaving the rest of your guests feeling like spare parts and wondering why you asked them to come! Introduce those guests that do not know each other so that no one will feel awkward about starting a conversation with a stranger. To break the ice, it is helpful to offer a little bit of background about each person, particularly something they may have in common, so that they immediately have something to talk to each other about.

## PARTY SUPPLIES

There are some useful pantry items and party paraphernalia you should always have on hand for match or movie nights, and unexpected visitors, to make sure you're recognised as the most successful hostess on the block.

### The List

- ✓ Cold beer
- ✓ Tonic water, fruit juices and other mixers
- ✓ Preferred drink ingredients for close friends
- ✓ Plenty of ice
- ✓ Salsa and tortilla chips
- ✓ Party dip packets
- ✓ Crackers and cheeses
- ✓ Mixed salted nuts
- ✓ Frozen party nibbles like sausage rolls, mini quiches, chicken strips
- ✓ Ice cream
- ✓ Chocolate biscuits and cookies
- ✓ Coffee
- ✓ Music system
- ✓ Glasses (inexpensive ones that can be replaced if broken)

- ✓ Partyware: platters, trays, cocktail napkins, dip bowls
- ✓ Good table linen
- ✓ Varied CD collection to match any mood
- ✓ At least two decks of cards
- ✓ Various board games
- ✓ Tissues, paper towels and extra rolls of toilet paper
- ✓ Large floor cushions or spare fold-out chairs
- ✓ Cocktail shaker
- ✓ Spare string of fairylights to pull out for a special event
- ✓ Plenty of side tables/coffee tables for guests to place their drinks
- ✓ Vases for fresh flowers
- ✓ Aluminium foil and plastic wrap for keeping food fresh

# THE INFORMAL SUPPER PARTY

This is by far the most enjoyable way to entertain, as the emphasis is not on the food but on the company. An informal supper party should be a relaxed affair, with minimum planning. You can throw the whole thing together with absolute ease and stylish flair if you follow just one basic rule. Keep It Simple. This is not the occasion to try out new and complicated recipes and impress your guests with your culinary expertise. There is nothing relaxing for your guests about watching a harried hostess slaving over a hot stove worrying about the finer details of French cuisine.

## *Easy Entertaining*

- ☑ Put a jug of Bloody Mary on the kitchen table and something simple to pick at – maybe a plate of toasts spread with a good farmhouse pate or some bread and olive oil.

- ☑ A one-pot casserole can be thrown together the previous day and will slow-cook on the lowest temperature in the oven while you are at work. All you need to do when you get home is slice some crusty bread as accompaniment and ladle it out into big bowls for rustic effect.

- ☑ For an impromptu gathering, fresh pasta takes only a few minutes to cook. Stir through some pesto, shave some parmesan over the top and serve with a salad.

- ☑ Cheeses on a wooden board, interspersed with piles of ripe seasonal fruit look gorgeous and are a great fuss-free dessert.

- ☑ Freshly brewed coffee and a bowl of dark chocolate broken into chunks is the perfect way to end the meal.

# KIDS PARTIES

Kid's parties can be a nightmare unless you are extremely organised. You could give the party a theme – just remember who has to make the costumes! The most important part of the proceedings is the birthday tea. You have to have a cake – as big and garishly iced as possible. Now is not the time to lay down the law about additives and sugar. Let them eat as much junk as they like – you can always put them to bed early and feed them broccoli every day until the next birthday party to make up for it.

Dealing with more than a handful of over-excited, sugar-high children can lead even the most patient mother to distraction. However, there are a few tips which will make the party go a little more smoothly.

## *Keeping Control*

- ✓ You don't have to invite every child in the class, a small handful of five or six, is a perfect number for a toddler's tea party. If you do invite every child in the class, have your party in the garden or get in extra help in the form of willing or gullible parents.

- ✓ Two hours is plenty long enough for children under five – you'll find it's long enough for you in any case

- ✓ Organise some games, but keep them simple and not too competitive.

- ✓ Don't feel you have to fill every moment of the party with an organised event or game. Small children are quite happy playing with toys, particularly other people's, so get a box of your kid's stuff ready in advance and that will keep them happy for at least half an hour.

- ✓ If any mother offers to stay, accept gratefully (and quickly, before she can change her mind), and put her to work immediately.

# SUNDAY LUNCH

Traditionally a time for family and friends, Sunday Lunch should really be as long and as lazy as possible. It does not need to be complicated. The thing most people get caught out by, is the timing of it all. The easiest way to get it right is to decide on a time to serve lunch and then work backwards. Give yourself 10 minutes extra breathing time when working it all out – no matter how organised you are, things will take a bit longer than you anticipate. That is just one of the unwritten rules about roast dinners, and most other household tasks actually, so as a Domestic Goddess you should be used to taking these little upsets in your stride.

## *Planning the Perfect Roast*

☑ Work out how long your joint needs to cook – the general rule is 20 minutes per pound of meat and then 20 minutes extra, although of course it depends on the type of meat and the temperature. Ask your butcher's advice if you are unsure.

☑ To eat at 2 pm, work the cooking time backwards from 1.30 pm to find out when the meat needs to go into the oven. Don't forget to take the meat out of the refrigerator well in advance to get it to room temperature before you start.

☑ If you are serving roast potatoes, which some might say is the best bit and surely the whole point of a roast dinner, they will take the next longest time to cook. Par-boil them first for a superior finish! They should be crunchy and chewy on the outside, while being soft and fluffy on the inside.

Apply the same principle to the vegetables and any other accompaniments you are serving, like stuffing or Yorkshire pudding. Calculate how long they take to cook and then work backwards from 2 pm to know when to put them in the oven.

 If you want to be super-organised and make sure absolutely nothing goes wrong, prepare everything in advance and write out a timetable.

 The gravy should be the last thing you do, using the meat juices from the roasting tray, when you have removed the joint to rest. Leave the gravy to bubble away merrily while you get someone else to lay the table and pour you a glass of wine.

 If you have been lucky enough to be invited to someone else's Sunday Lunch, take a bottle of wine and offer to wash up afterwards.

# DRINKS PARTY

Throwing a drinks party is a great way to entertain without the worry of catering for a lot of people. However, it isn't necessarily easier than having a formal dinner party – there are still lots of things to consider.

## GET THE PARTY STARTED

Drinks parties can be held early in the evening before dinner, so you could expect to have guests arrive at 6pm or thereabouts and stay for a couple of hours. These affairs are called cocktail parties and were all the rage in the 1950's. Happily, the serving of cocktails has fallen back into favour again, but sherry, champagne or wine is still quite usual. For the beginner, or the hostess short of time, the attraction of the cocktail party is its brevity – leaving you the rest of the evening to tidy up and eat your supper in peace.

Drinks parties are also common later in the evening after dinner and tend to go on much longer, perhaps with some dancing. It is usual to serve some light snacks, canapes or finger food at both types of drinks parties – an especially good idea when you are laying on lots of alcohol but not a proper meal.

## COCKTAIL CLASSICS

I can think of nothing more fabulous than mixing some glamorous cocktails for a pre-dinner party and it is always memorable to do something a little out of the ordinary. You could pick a classic – like Margarita or Martini – and mix them in advance, served in elegant glass pitchers. Or you could go the whole hog and have a fully-stocked bar where people can make their own. If you can afford to hire a barman for the evening, so much the better, but you may have to settle for The Husband taking on the role armed with a book of cocktail recipes.

# Getting the Party Started

✓   Ice is essential, and lots of it. Fill some buckets with it for chilling wine and champagne as well as for serving drinks 'on the rocks'.

✓   You'll need an assortment of glasses if you are going to offer different types of drinks, but you can probably manage with wine glasses, hi-balls, and tumblers. Cocktail glasses would be a glamorous bonus.

✓   Don't underestimate how many glasses you will need, guests have an irritating habit of putting them down and 'losing' them or deciding to switch their choice of drink part-way through the evening.

✓   If you are only serving wine or champagne during a two-hour party, you will probably need about one bottle for every two people, but it's better to overestimate than run out, or everyone will leave early.

✓   If you intend to offer a basic bar, you'll need vodka, whisky, wines and beer. If you are going for the whole shooting match, add gin, tequila, rum, bourbon, vermouth, sherry and brandy.

✓   Mixers are essential, including orange juice, soda, tonic, ginger ale, cola, tomato juice, Tabasco, lemons, limes, horseradish, Worcestershire sauce. Chuck in a few of those little paper umbrellas, some cherries and cocktail sticks for kitsch retro appeal.

✓   You may want to have the telephone number of a taxi company to hand for anyone looking the worse for wear at the end of the party.

# THE FORMAL DINNER

The idea of hosting a formal dinner should not make you come out in a cold sweat! (Not that you would do anything so vulgar anyway, but you might feel a flutter of apprehension . . .) The rules are very simple, and really not that different from any other type of party, except of course that the food takes centre stage.

Deciding on the menu is the tricky bit. Consider how well you can cook, what help you have, what your budget is, the time of the year and just how formal you wish to be. A starter and main course, followed by pudding and cheese, and lastly coffee, works perfectly well, and can be made as simple or as complicated as you like. Bear in mind the season – you do not want to serve a heavy roast dinner on a hot summer's evening. Likewise, if it is a chilly winter's night, your guests will appreciate something more substantial and warming than a salad.

## SEATING PLANS

A word of warning on the guest list– many hostesses see drawing up a guest list and arranging a seating plan as an opportunity to play cupid to their single friends. This is potentially dangerous. Whilst it might be an amusing diversion to attempt to match-make, it rarely goes according to plan. It puts your guests under extreme pressure. Even if you do not directly tell them of your intentions, you will be unable to help yourself putting them under intense surveillance throughout the meal (so you can check on progress) and you will probably make pointed remarks highlighting their individual benefits. Don't do it. Resist the temptation. There is no harm in seating one of your single girlfriends next to a particularly charming unattached young man, but leave it at that. If they like the look of each other, they'll sort it out. If they need any encouragement, you can give them hand the following day.

## *Planning a Dinner*

 You want your guests to positively swoon with delight when they see the dining table. Start with a freshly laundered cloth – white always looks classically elegant, and table napkins to match.

 Polish your cutlery, even if it is not silver, until it shines.

 Avoid the temptation to place a large centrepiece in the middle of the table. You do want your guests to be able to see each other across the table.

 Candles are essential to provide atmosphere, but again, be careful where they are placed so that diners do not run the risk of setting their arm on fire as they reach for the salt.

 When you are working out your seating plan, there are a few things to consider. Gone are the days when dinner parties in private houses seated guests in order of social rank, but you do need to ensure that nobody feels left out. Avoid bunching together people who know each other terribly well. It is also customary to alternate the sexes round the table and split up married couples.

 The priority of the hostess, throughout the evening, is the wellbeing and enjoyment of her guests. Prepare as much as you can in advance, especially if you are not hiring staff to help and will be doing everything yourself.

 Limit the amount of time that you absent yourself from your guests, as they may well wonder why they bothered to come at all if you spend the whole evening in the kitchen. However amazing the food is, your guests would prefer the attention of their hostess.

Finally, be charming, witty and bright and strive to appear unruffled, serene and in control at all times. Wear a killer dress and smile.

# KITCHEN DISASTERS

What do you do when the souffle won't rise and the soup has curdled? With your unique sense of style and panache, you just need to take every kitchen disaster in your stride and make sure you still pull off a first-rate party.

## *Rescuing Dinner*

☑ Stick with a tried and tested recipe that you are familiar with when you are having people round to dinner. Don't try to be clever by cooking new and complicated recipes and this will decrease your chances of incurring a kitchen disaster in the first place.

☑ Keep calm and don't panic if something does go wrong. Kitchen disasters are rarely as calamitous as they first appear. Think logically about how you can save the course that is ruined. Use your store cupboard or freezer supplies if necessary.

☑ If you drop something on the floor, this is not the time to be squeamish. If no-one saw you, scoop it up – you know how gleamingly clean your floors are.

☑ There is no need to draw attention to your mistakes by apologising for them. It is highly unlikely anyone will notice them and if they do, it would be extremely rude to point them out.

☑ If your dish is excessively salty, try peeling a large potato, chopping into chunks and throwing it into the pan. Remove when soft – it should have absorbed the extra salt.

☑ To remove excess fat or grease from dishes such as casseroles, soups or gravy, try placing a slice of bread on the top and it should absorb the excess.

When baking, line your tins with greaseproof or baking paper before pouring in the mixture to avoid them sticking to your bakeware and to ease their swift and easy removal.

 If cakes or biscuits do break up as you're removing them, it's not a problem – add whipped cream and fresh fruit and stir through loosely. Serve in a glass for a modern take on a classic trifle.

 You can mash or blend overcooked vegetables in the food processor, with some butter and a dash of cream and serve fashionably pureed.

 Adding a little paste of cornstarch and water can save a curdled cream sauce from the dustbin.

 Try adding a teaspoon or two of olive oil if your chocolate suddenly goes hard and grainy during melting.

# ADVANCED ENTERTAINING

There are some occasions where you will feel especially under pressure. Perhaps the boss is coming to dinner or the in-laws, or it might be The Husband's birthday or perhaps a Christmas party. There are a few things you could try, if you have the confidence and the time and are feeling brave, that will secure your position as the Perfect Hostess and take your entertaining from the merely marvellous to the magical.

There are a few simple rules to follow when throwing a party to ensure that it is always a smashing success and that your guests are falling over themselves to secure an invitation to a future gathering.

# *Party Pointers*

 Consider a simple colour scheme for the evening. White and gold look elegant together, or chocolate and cream, or lilac and silver. Be creative. Candles, flowers, tableware, linen – co-ordinate the lot and give your party a feeling of continuity.

 Avoid electric lighting, opt for candlelight instead. Not only does everyone look their best in the subtle flickering glow but it creates a warm and intimate feeling. Try grouping together a collection of candles in several areas around the room. You may want to avoid the scented type as they can be a little overpowering. You don't want anything to detract from the delicious smells of your meal.

 Like candles, I think you can afford to go overboard with flowers to no ill effect. Put some in the bathroom, hallway, sitting and dining rooms. Even have some in the kitchen to cheer you while you cook.

 It is a nice touch to hand write name cards for each guest. Personalise them with a favourite quotation or even a jolly character sketch.

 Similarly, a handwritten menu can be a lovely detail which your guests will appreciate. It whets the appetite and can be a great conversation starter while people are waiting for their first course.

 Rather than arranging napkins in intricate folds on the plate, or worse, in a glass – which looks fussy and a little dated now – try simply rolling or folding neatly and securing with a pretty piece of ribbon and a single bloom.

☑ The mark of the perfect hostess is her attention to detail. A quirky or unusual touch will make your parties memorable for all the right reasons. Develop your own individual hallmark – a signature dish or decorating style that people will come to recognise as your own. Little surprises will delight and wow your guests and your parties will be the most talked about social events of the year!

# HOW TO ENJOY YOUR OWN PARTIES

As anyone who has ever hosted an event knows, throwing a party is a job. But once the first guest arrives, the best hostess relaxes and remembers why she wanted to have the party in the first place: because they're fun!

## *Entertaining Short-cuts*

✓ Try a buffet. After the initial set-up, you are then free to socialise instead of being stuck in the kitchen keeping an eye on the next course. Just allow your guests to fill their plates before you sample your delicious dishes.

✓ If you're throwing a large dinner party there is no shame in hiring some help in the kitchen. All great chefs still have a sous-chef after all.

✓ You could also consider hiring waiters so you can mingle freely. If there is a teenager in the neighbourhood, consider hiring him or her for the evening to refill glasses and distribute canapés, not to mention removing used plates and glassware.

✓ Go potluck. Ask guests to bring a dish or drink so your preparation time (and budget) is cut back.

✓ Give guests roles, be it the game master, grill king, doorman or barmaid. They'll be delighted to help out.

✓ Cheat on the food. Buy take-away, hide the containers (consider driving the evidence to a nearby tip), and dress up the food to avoid detection. From chicken curry to guacamole, restaurants, delicatessens and specialist shops supply simple or exotic foods for your gathering. Doctor up your dishes with spices and garnish with fresh herbs.

# HOSTESS SUCCESS

Thorough preparation and planning means the party will run on autopilot, leaving the hostess to relax and enjoy spending time with her guests. Here are the top ten rules to Perfect Hostess Success:

## Top Ten Rules to Hostess Success

**1**  Glasses should always be full.

**2**  Lighting should be low and soft.

**3**  Food should be varied and plentiful, and spread throughout the party area.

**4**  Music should play continuously at a volume suitable for conversation (unless dancing is afoot).

**5**  The perfect hostess should dress the part. It is your party and on this occasion there is no such thing as being overdressed.

**6**  The perfect hostess should also make the host shine, however unpolished he may be.

**7**  The host and hostess should divide and conquer. Split up and reconnect at the end of the evening to recap over a nightcap.

**8**  Introduce guests with an interesting fact about each other so a conversation is easily started.

**9**  Mingle. Avoid lingering too long in one place or with one person.

**10**  Don't sweat the small stuff. If someone breaks or damages something, smile and reassure your guest. Belongings can be repaired more easily than hurt feelings.

# 7

# FAMILY
# MATTERS

We are all encumbered with assorted baggage on the relationship front and it can make life a little complicated. It is eminently sensible to approach family matters in much the same way that you tackle your house; you need to have a strategy for dealing with The Husband, The Children and more importantly, The In-laws . . .

# ARE YOU READY?

As we know, a Domestic Goddess is equipped to deal with every domestic eventuality. However, there are some accidents that no amount of culinary tips, a stockpile of stain removers and a comprehensive understanding of fabric care symbols can address.

Life's little surprises have a way of creeping up on you without warning. That's why they are surprises. Sometimes they are most welcome – finding a ten pound note down the back of the sofa, for instance, or winning a lifetime's supply of chocolate in a competition. Some are less welcome – your mother-in-law arriving unannounced on your doorstep with her suitcase perhaps, or being knocked over by a bus. Now, whether or not you consider an unplanned pregnancy to be of the welcome or unwelcome variety, it is always a better idea to plan your family and get used to the idea slowly.

---

## Getting Ready for Baby

✔ If you're not sure how The Husband feels about having kids, see how he reacts to the small children that you encounter in your lives. Does he smile at them wistfully, or screw up his face with revulsion?

✔ Watch his reaction when holding babies at family gatherings. Does he cuddle them close or hold them gingerly at arm's length as if handling an unexploded bomb? (A note of caution – this is not always a reliable way to gauge his enthusiasm. All men display nervousness of some degree or another when holding small babies. They worry, quite rightly, that they may drop them. Check to see whether he has the child the right way up. If he is holding the baby upside-down, he is probably not ready yet for his own just yet.)

Be realistic about your current circumstances. While there's rarely an ideal time to have a child, the two of you should be on the same page about the logistics, emotional readiness, and timeline before conceiving.

 Think about a timeline. Unless you have medical reasons to hurry things along, take your time discussing your plans. Let yourselves get used to the idea of a child before committing to the real thing.

 Don't turn the spare room into a nursery over-night or buy a boatload of pregnancy books or baby toys – this will send The Husband screaming for the hills. Break him in gently to the idea.

 While you may be nervous about the responsibility of parenthood, you should both also feel truly excited by it. Once you have a child, it's forever. Make sure that you – and your relationship – are ready for it.

# CHILD SAFETY

When the new baby arrives, you will find time goes very quickly. Before long your little one will be toddling and starting to explore the world around him. Before you know it he'll be into every cupboard, poking fingers into electric sockets, posting toast into the DVD player and retuning the television. Suddenly every sharp corner, the staircase, a slippery floor becomes a potential health hazard to your intrepid explorer. It pays to be prepared and put child safety measures in place before he gets to this stage.

## *Baby-Proofing Your Home*

☑ Cleaning materials and household chemicals should be locked away or at least in a cupboard high up out of reach. The same goes for medicines, sharp knives, scissors and kitchen implements, also cigarette lighters, matches and alcohol.

☑ Get plastic safety catches for all your kitchen cupboards. Moulded plastic shields can be fixed on sharp corners where he is likely to hurt himself, especially on the edges of coffee tables. Special guards designed for video and TVs and covers for electrical sockets will prevent little fingers fiddling.

☑ When you are cooking, make sure that handles on saucepans are turned inwards so junior can't reach up and pull them off the stove.

☑ Don't leave electrical flexes trailing, from irons or kettles for instance, or he'll pull those too and could burn himself quite nastily.

☑ Stair gates are an essential part of your child safety kit and are incredibly useful all over the house, not just at the top and bottom of the staircase. Use them in the bedroom doorway so that if your child masters the neat trick of jumping out of the cot all the time, he or she can't go wondering unsupervised around the house.

- Playpens are also handy, especially ones that open out and double as a room divider. These are also great to use in the garden so your child can safely enjoy some fresh air.

- If you have a gas, electric or open fire, you must have a fire guard. Make sure it stands well back from the fireplace or it can get too hot, and guards with a top cover like a lid are extra safe, preventing the more adventurous child from actually climbing over.

- Don't forget to put small items out of reach. At this stage, your toddler will put everything in his mouth and the danger of choking is very real.

- Never change your baby's nappy on a raised surface when he is old enough to roll himself over.

- Be extra vigilant at bath times. Run the cold water first and check the temperature. Use a non-slip rubber mat. Get everything you will need ready beforehand.

- Never leave him unattended in the bath for even a second, even with an older sibling, as small children can drown very quickly in only a few centimetres of water.

- Don't overlook your outdoor space. Ensure all fencing and gates are secure, especially if your garden is near a road. Look out for loose panels, broken planks and exposed nails. Sandpits will need watertight and cat-proof lids.

- Ponds are a particular point of concern. Small children and water don't mix well. Fit a pond guard (a wire mesh that sits just below the water line) or fill it in.

# NAPPY TRAIN THE HUSBAND

Your man is a child at heart. Like a boy, he loves it when you make him a sandwich, run him a bath, surprise him with a treat, and care for him when he's sick. In most relationships, the woman is the primary nurturer, caring for both the home and the relationship in an instinctively maternal way. So it's no surprise that when a man resists the idea of children, there's often an unspoken reason: he worries about losing your nurturing attention; he's afraid of having to share your love and your energy; and he's resistant to the idea of not being the centre of your world. Who can blame him?

## REASSURE HIM

Remember that you have the ability to ease his fears, even when he doesn't verbalise them. Assure him, at every turn, that you have enough love to go around and that you will still make time for your relationship as well as the kids. Let him know that you can establish ground rules and traditions as a couple to make sure you keep the romance alive, even after you have children – from committing to a monthly date night to ensuring a bedtime routine that allows for intimacy.

## GET AWAY FROM IT ALL

Admittedly, your schedule will become erratic and busy with the introduction of children into your lives. That's why it's imperative that you carve out time to spend together. Treat it as you would an appointment with a client. And if at all possible, get out of the house. Hire a babysitter or ask a relative or friend to watch the kids, go out to dinner and stare into each other's eyes. Go to a movie and snuggle up to him in the dark. Take a walk on the beach and enjoy a scream- and tantrum-free zone as you listen to the waves.

# TIME TOGETHER . . .

Even before you have children, you can reassure your man that your relationship won't take a back seat. Talk about what's most important to you as you get ready for parenthood, the rules to lay down and the questions that will accompany all your important decisions. Use this list as a springboard to useful discussion on the subject. Don't get too frustrated if you don't meet all of your goals all of the time – what's important is that you can discuss it with your partner and see the way forward.

## *After we have a baby, it is important that we . . .*

| | |
|---|---|
| Still travel | What kinds of places can we go that are both appealing to us and baby-friendly? |
| Have regular dates | How often? |
| Set a firm bedtime for our children | Should we also establish a set time that we go to the bedroom? |
| Keep the house in order | Is a maid or cleaning service an option, and will everyone do their bit? |
| Maintain close relationships with our friends | How can we ensure this? |
| Maintain some independence | Should each parent have a monthly "free night" to get out of the house, see friends, or pursue hobbies? |
| Are still dedicated to a demanding career | What compromises can be made for the sake of everyone's sanity? |

# . . . TIME APART

The key to happiness and longevity in a successful relationship is to make sure both of you keep some time for yourselves, and pursue separate interests and hobbies. As much as you love that husband of yours, it's unrealistic and unreasonable to expect to spend every hour of every day with him. Forget about how trapped he will feel for just a minute. Take a moment to think first about yourself. Imagine if he joined you for every activity. While he may come in handy when you want someone to carry your bags, resist the urge to include him in all of your activities. Make the time to maintain your interests and the space to spread your wings.

Do take an interest in his hobbies as well. There's no way to put this gently. Sports matter to him. . . and therefore they matter to you. Take a little time to grasp some basics about various sports so that you can talk intelligently about his favourite team and even join him as an armchair fan.

## *Sharing His Hobbies*

✓ The first step in embracing his zeal for sports is to respect his interest and level of enthusiasm. Do not scoff at it, or refer to it as a waste of time and money, that will not go down well.

✓ Save questions until half time or the ad break. If you pester him, he will ignore you or even snap at you. Don't take it personally. Just learn from the first time and wait for a lull to chat.

✓ Now that you've dipped your toe into his sport, get to know a few players on his team. You'll begin to perk up when they are playing or do something particularly well. You may even actually start rooting for them.

# THE IN-LAWS

Ahhh, family. What used to be a safe haven has now, occasionally, become a den of doubt, if not outright opposition. And not just from his side. You may find your own parents are just as trying when it comes to your relationship. Your mother, for example, may well be your closest confidante. You may tell her everything. She wants you to be happy and is thrilled that you've settled down with a good man. But she has only your best interests at heart. So like your friends, take care about over-sharing with your mum. At the slightest sign that he isn't treating you as you deserve – even if it's an isolated incident – your mother will find ways to discourage the relationship (if she secretly thinks you can do better) or to defend his actions (if she is worried about you being single again). Be discreet in confiding things about your relationship. Even better, ask questions about how your mother has dealt with the issues surrounding living with a man. As she shares her experiences, she'll feel appreciated, but you can still remain vague about your problems or concerns.

## STAYING NEUTRAL

It may take a while for The Husband and your mum to warm to each other. Don't take sides. This is a no-win situation, as you love them both and will either defend their actions or try to convince each of the other's qualities. They must discover what kind of relationship is comfortable for both of them. All you can do is give them time and opportunities. Your family believes you to be a precious pearl, because you are. It will be hard to convince your parents that your husband is your equal. You must give them time to discover the wonderful qualities about him that you love . . . and vice versa. And they will. And if they don't there's not much you can do about it. Instead, turn your attention towards wooing The In-laws.

## *Wooing the In-laws*

☑ Don't hit them over the head with attention and fuss. Simply rely on your impeccable manners to see you through.

☑ Take their lead on physical and verbal intimacy; that is, hug them if they hug you, call them by their first name if they invite you to do so. Respecting their boundaries and comfort level will go a long way to endearing you to them.

☑ Compliment their home, play with their pet, clean your plate, no matter how questionable a cook your mother-in-law is.

☑ When you invite them into your home, make sure they feel welcome. Ask them for their advice on home-making or interior decoration or communicating with your husband. This will subtly drive home the point that you are not trying to take their son away or competing with them for his affection. Rather, you are creating a home for him where they too can be comfortable spending time.

☑ But not so comfortable that they want to live with you! That may wreak havoc on hearth and home, so you generally want to avoid this at all costs. Don't be swayed by guilt or passive disapproval.

☑ Seek out time with your mother-in-law, and ask her to share baby photos or childhood stories about him. This will demonstrate that while you love him, you don't know everything about him. You certainly haven't known him as long or as well as she has, so respect that.

☑ Show an interest in her outside of her being your beloved's mother. You may find that you like her and would seek out her friendship, regardless of your relationship with her son. But you have a link to start from: you love the same man. Build upon that foundation and the relationship will grow from there.

# WHEN THE TOYS GET ON TOP

There is no easy answer to the tyranny of toys. They can, quite literally, take over your house and your life. Unfortunately, there are no self-help group meetings one can attend to learn to cope with the destruction toys can wreak on your life and those around you. The problem is perennial, so you will just have to accept it, but there are however one or two things you can do to limit the chaos.

## *Taming the Toys*

☑ Be very strict about just how many toys you buy for your children or they are given. When they are young, and growing out of everything so quickly, ask for a new winter coat from Granny instead.

☑ Gather all their toys in one place. Do this when they are asleep or out of the house, or they will try and 'help' and you'll end up keeping broken dolls with only one leg, jigsaws with pieces missing, or cars with only two wheels.

☑ Be ruthless. Arm your self with a cardboard box and a black bin liner, and start sorting into piles. It is then easy to see what is broken, incomplete or no longer age-relevant. Throw away the rubbish, and put any toys that are still good but too childish, into the box. Take the box to the local hospital and leave it there.

☑ Under no circumstances get sentimental about things and do not let your children know you are doing this. Trust me, it will only end in tears – theirs and yours.

☑ Devise a storage system. Large plastic tubs or buckets, the huge sturdy type that builders use to mix concrete in, are very useful for your child's never-ending supply of toys.

Creating storage solutions will also make it easier for the kids to put their toys away after use, if the receptacle requires no opening or closing – merely the scooping up of armfuls and dropping in. Get several in bright colours and stick labels on them or if the kids are too young to read, cut out pictures of the relevant toy from magazines.

 An empty trunk or sideboard will hold several buckets if you are sick of seeing the children's stuff. There is something very liberating, however short-lived, about clearing your sitting room of all the evidence and enjoying a 'child-free' evening.

 Be tough with your rules about toys. The children must put one lot of toys away before they get out another bucket. They must always, always tidy up before they go to bed. They are never too young to start.

# PLAYING NURSE

We are not talking about bedroom games here. It is a rather more serious affair. Sooner or later, The Husband or The Children are going to get ill – most likely they will all succumb at the exact same time – and it will be up to you to look after them all.

Firstly you need decide whether medical treatment is necessary. Some illnesses or ailments, such as colds, can be treated at home without the need for medical intervention. Obviously a Domestic Goddess's nursing skills only go so far, and in an emergency situation, you should call the emergency services. In many cases, especially in the case of very young babies, and older children with excessively high temperatures which may lead to febrile convulsions, it is better always to be safe than sorry and call your GP. Check with your health visitor for up-to-date advice and recommendations and paste it inside the lid of your first aid box, so you can check the guidelines when you are worried about your child.

It is important to keep high standards of hygiene, particularly when there is an ill person in the house. Washing hands after using the bathroom, before and after preparing food and before eating are habits that we should all get into, being especially vigilant when a member of the family is unwell.

## FIRST AID

It is essential to have a well-stocked first-aid kit in your home, with some basic medical supplies. Your nursing skills should at least extend as far as basic first aid and doling out plasters. Store your kit in a secure place where small children can not get at it, but where everyone else in the house will have easy access. And don't forget to tell everyone where it is! Remember to keep it fully-stocked at all times, this means replacing something when you have used it, as you never know when an emergency may occur.

It is also a good idea to enclose some basic first aid principles – either handwritten, or even a first aid manual. In the case of common emergencies such as burns, heart-attack, unconsciousness, allergies, bleeding or stopping breathing, the information is there to help you and your family tackle a crisis with confidence.

*First Aid Box Essentials*

- ✓ adhesive tape
- ✓ sterile gauze
- ✓ different sized bandages
- ✓ elastic bandage
- ✓ antiseptic wipes
- ✓ antibiotic ointment
- ✓ antiseptic solution
- ✓ painkillers

- ✓ hydrocortisone cream
- ✓ sharp scissors
- ✓ safety pins
- ✓ tweezers
- ✓ disposable instant cold packs
- ✓ calamine lotion
- ✓ thermometer
- ✓ plastic gloves

# HOMEMADE REMEDIES

There are all sorts of things you can do at home to make your children, and your husband, more comfortable when they are feeling run down. Here are some home remedies which are really effective:

## *Home Remedies*

☑ It is important to keep children's fluids up, particularly if they have a fever or are suffering from vomiting, diarrhoea or a cold. It is wise to stick to water if they have an unsettled stomach as anything too acidic may well irritate and make them feel worse. Only allow little sips, but do so constantly so they do not get dehydrated. Otherwise, fruit juice, diluted for younger children is a great source of vitamin C.

☑ To reduce a fever, try sponging with tepid water, removing heavy bedclothes and an electric fan on a cold setting can help. Don't allow them to get too chilly though.

☑ A few drops of lavender oil in a warm bath will soothe fractious children before sleep, or place a few drops in a bowl of hot water in their bedroom, out of reach, so they can breathe in the calming aroma. Similarly, a few drops of eucalyptus oil will help decongest blocked nasal passages.

☑ Croup or hacking coughs can be alleviated by placing your child on your knee in a steamy environment. Run a hot bath and sit together on a chair, perhaps with a book, for a good ten minutes.

☑ Prune or grape juice is great for sorting out constipated children and a hi-fibre cereal for breakfast will keep them regular.

☑ Nappy rash can be calmed by adding some bicarbonate of soda to the bath water.

Peppermints can alleviate indigestion and nausea, as can peppermint tea. Ginger, raw and grated in hot water, or even commercial ginger ale, does the same thing. Also good for car sickness.

 Not only is garlic fantastic for sorting out colds and flu, it is a brilliant remedy for ear ache. Warm some garlic oil and drip into the afflicted ear twice a day.

# INDEX